THE REMBRANDT
DRAWINGS AND ETCHINGS

REMBRANDT: ETCHING OF CLEMENT DE JONGHE
H. 251

THE
REMBRANDT DRAWINGS
AND ETCHINGS

WITH CRITICAL REASSIGNMENTS TO PUPILS
AND FOLLOWERS

BY

JOHN C. VAN DYKE

PROFESSOR OF THE HISTORY OF ART AND ARCHÆOLOGY IN RUTGERS UNIVERSITY,
SOMETIME LECTURER AT PRINCETON, COLUMBIA, AND HARVARD UNIVERSITIES;
AUTHOR OF "REMBRANDT AND HIS SCHOOL," "A HISTORY OF PAINTING," "OLD
DUTCH AND FLEMISH MASTERS," "NEW GUIDES TO OLD MASTERS," ETC.

CHARLES SCRIBNER'S SONS
NEW YORK · LONDON
1927

COPYRIGHT, 1927, BY
CHARLES SCRIBNER'S SONS

Printed in the United States of America

DEDICATED

TO

GEORGIANA L. McCLELLAN

PREFACE

Four years ago in sending forth a volume[1] on the paintings in the Rembrandt *œuvre* I intimated that I should have something to say later about the drawings and the etchings. They are part and parcel of the general Rembrandt output, and absolutely essential to any argument about the paintings. For the same artistic personalities appear throughout the entire work—paintings, drawings, and etchings—and have merely to be indicated to be recognized. The only question has been as to when and where the drawings and etchings should be dealt with. I have thought they could be better presented in a separate book. Hence this volume, which should be regarded as a supplementary and concluding volume to the one on the paintings.

The same method of identification and assignment is pursued herein as therein. It need not be elaborated again just here, but I may say that neither here nor there have I made assignments without giving the reasons therefor. I have placed my whole method upon the table for any one and every one to examine. No doubt there are instances where it fails to function, but at least there is no concealment about it. Nor throughout the whole book, any pretence to finality or freedom from error. It is not possible, with or without a method, for me (or for that matter any one else) to question the attributions of say 300 pictures, 200 etchings, and 500 drawings without making mistakes. These errors may furnish catch points for the opposition, and those with a genius for picking up pins may make much of them, but my contention that the Rembrandt *œuvre* is an aggregation of the entire Rembrandt school, and needs to be broken into its component parts, will not be invalidated thereby. I shall exemplify that contention once more in this volume. If I can indicate a general direction, no matter how rough the trail may be, there will be others to follow it and open up a thoroughfare.

In the study of the Rembrandt drawings the student will have many volumes of reproductions to aid him. Perhaps the most notable set of reproductions is the ten-folio work of Lippmann and DeGroot, published in 1899–1909. Selected drawings are reproduced in Neumann, *Rem-*

---

[1] *Rembrandt and His School*, New York, 1923.

brandts Handzeichnungen; Kleinmann, *Handzeichnungen alter Meister der höllandischen Schule, Haarlem;* Bell, *Drawings of Rembrandt;* Michel, *Life of Rembrandt.* The volumes containing reproductions of Rembrandt drawings in different museums are chiefly Freise & Lilienfeld, *Rembrandts Handzeichnungen,* Amsterdam and Berlin, 1924; Dresden, 1925; Munich, *Kupferstichkabinet, Handzeichnungen alter Meister, ed. W. Schmidt,* 1884– 1900; Paris, *Les Dessins du Louvre par H. de Chennevières,* 1895; Frankfort, *Handzeichnungen alter Meister im Städelschen Kunstinstitut,* 1908– ; Térey, *Zeichnungen von Rembrandt im Budapester Museen,* Leipzig, 1909; Kruse, *Die Zeichnungen Rembrandts,* Stockholm Museum; Falck, *Kopferstichsammlungen,* Stockholm Museum; Schönbrunner & Meder, *Handzeichnungen, alter Meister aus der Albertina,* etc., 1896; Heseltine, *Original Drawings of Rembrandt in Heseltine Collection; Teekeningen van Rembrandt in de Verzameling C. Hofstede de Groot te's Gravenhage,* Haarlem, 1909. All of these volumes of drawings are put together with little or no discrimination of the many different styles among the drawings, though they usually recount the documentary and traditional evidence for them. They should be regarded as reproductions of the combined works of Rembrandt and his school. A work now in process of publication by Doctor Valentiner, *Die Handzeichnungen Rembrandts,* the first volume issued in 1925, contains many illustrations not published elsewhere, and is a valuable compilation. The reproductions (464 in the first volume) are excellent, and will be referred to by number in this volume. The notes by Doctor Valentiner are critical and should be read by the student though they are diametrically opposed to my own views and to the conclusions of this volume.

The catalogues of Rembrandt drawings practically began with Vosmaer, who, in his first edition, gave 320 numbers. In his second edition this had mounted to 700. Dutuit, following Vosmaer in 1883, published a supplementary volume of the drawings, and Michel, in 1893, gave a list of 900. All the galleries and museums with their holdings were not included in these lists. It remained for Doctor Hofstede de Groot to arrange the most definitive catalogue of the drawings—*Die Handzeichnungen Rembrandts,* Haarlem, 1906—that has yet appeared. It is out of print and scarce but is quite necessary to the student because it gives much of the literary and hearsay evidence regarding some 1,613 drawings assigned (with occasional doubtings) to Rembrandt. The work by Doctor Valentiner, referred to above, supplements but does not supersede that of Doctor de Groot.

The etchings have received perhaps greater consideration than the drawings, but their critical status is still decidedly uncertain. The early catalogues of Gersaint, Daulby, Bartsch, Claussin, Middleton-Wake, Seidlitz, Dutuit, list almost everything, beginning with the inventory of Clement de Jonghe, containing 74 plates, and adding enough plates discovered in recent years to make up 300 or more, all told. The latter-day catalogues and comments on the Rembrandt etchings by Seymour Haden, Hamerton, Holmes, Colvin, and others have more critical value, especially the brochure of Seymour Haden, entitled *Catalogue of the Etched Work of Rembrandt*, London, 1877, which sets forth the view of a practical etcher on the Rembrandt etchings and their many contradictory styles.

Numerous reproductions of the etchings have been published, but again with little or no discrimination or critical acumen. The folios of Blanc, Dutuit, and Rovinski are largely *omnium gatherums*. A good set of reproductions is published by Singer, *Rembrandts Radierungen*, 3 folios. A selected set of etchings is also given by Bell (London). But the most available and least expensive work is by Hind, *Rembrandt's Etchings*, London, 1912 (a second edition, 1923). Because of its availability, and because of the author's knowledge of his materials and manifest fairness in comment, I shall use the Hind book herein, referring to it by number throughout this volume.

The reproductions of neither the etchings nor the drawings can be accepted in a final analysis. In many details of line, tone, tint, ink, paper, they are defective. They must be considered merely as a compromise, and in every important matter the original should be consulted. The original drawings are to be found, for the greater part, in the European museums. The collections of etchings are more widely scattered, but perhaps the best impressions are to be seen in such institutions as the Ryks Museum, Amsterdam, or the British Museum, London, or the Morgan Library, New York.

The illustrations in this volume are merely selected memoranda to aid the memory, or by juxtaposition suggest analogies or resemblances. Taken in groups they should tend to establish artistic personalities not only by pointing out likenesses, but also differences, one from another. If they do that much they will have fulfilled expectations. In number they are, of course, by no means complete, and the student should consider them merely as examples (or samples) of the work of the different men. The whole work of each man, in painting, drawing, and etching, should be brought together from the works I have cited.

Acknowledgments are made to the trustees of the New York Public Library for permission to reproduce from their collections practically all the etchings in this volume; also to Mr. A. M. Hind for permission to reproduce from his volumes on the Rembrandt etchings; also to the Deutsche Verlags-Anstalt, Stuttgart, for permission to reproduce Rembrandt paintings and drawings from their Klassiker der Kunst series; to the British Museum, the Ryks Museum, and other European museums for the use of materials; and to many connoisseurs and collectors who have placed photographs at my disposal.

JOHN C. VAN DYKE.

RUTGERS UNIVERSITY, 1927.

CONTENTS

ILLUSTRATIONS

ILLUSTRATIONS

ILLUSTRATIONS

ABBREVIATIONS USED IN REFERENCE

Bartsch.	*Catalogue Raisonné*, Vienna, 1797.
Bauch.	Bauch, *Jakob Adriaensz Backer*, Berlin, 1926.
Bell.	Malcolm Bell, *Drawings of Rembrandt van Rhijn*, London.
Blanc.	Blanc, *L'Œuvre complet de Rembrandt*, Paris, 1880.
Chennevières.	Chennevières, *Les Dessins du Louvre*, Paris, 1895.
Coppier.	Coppier, *Les Eaux Fortes de Rembrandt*, Paris, 1922.
Dutuit.	Dutuit, *L'Œuvre complet de Rembrandt*, 1883.
Falck.	Falck, *Kopferstichsammlungen*, Stockholm Museum.
Frankfort.	Frankfort, *Handzeichnungen alter Meister im Städelschen Kunstinstitut*, 1908– .
Haden.	Seymour Haden, *Catalogue of the Etched Work of Rembrandt*, 1879.
Heseltine.	*Dessins de Rembrandt de la Collection J. P. Heseltine de Londres*, Amsterdam, 1913.
Hind, B. M.	A. M. Hind, *Catalogue of Drawings by Dutch and Flemish Artists in the British Museum*, London, 1915.
Hind.	A. M. Hind, *Rembrandt's Etchings*, vol. II, London, 1912 and 1923.
Hind, D.	A. M. Hind, *Rembrandt's Etchings*, vol. I, London, 1912 and 1923.
H. de G.	Hofstede de Groot, *Die Handzeichnungen Rembrandts*, Haarlem, 1906.
K.K.	*Klassiker der Kunst Series, Rembrandt*, Stuttgart, 1908.
K.K.Supp.	*Klassiker der Kunst Series, Rembrandt Supplement*.
Kleinmann.	Kleinmann, *Handzeichnungen alter Meister der holländischen Schule*.
Kruse.	Kruse, *Die Zeichnungen Rembrandts und seiner Schule im National Museum, Stockholm*, Haag, 1920.
Lilienfeld.	Lilienfeld, *Rembrandt's Handzeichnungen*, 3 vols. Vol. I, Amsterdam, 1912; vol. II, Berlin, 1914; vol. III, Dresden, 1925.
Lippmann.	Lippmann-Hofstede de Groot, *Handzeichnungen von Rembrandt Harmenz van Rijn*, 1899–1909.
Meder.	Schönbrunner und Meder, *Handzeichnungen von Rembrandt aus der Albertina, Vienna*, Paris, 1906; Neue Folge, 1922.
Michel.	Michel, *Rembrandt, His Life, His Work and His Time*, 2 vols., New York, 1894.
Middleton.	Middleton-Wake, *Catalogue of the Etched Work of Rembrandt*, 1878.
Neumann.	Neumann, *Rembrandts Handzeichnungen*, München, 1921.
Pauli.	Pauli, *Zeichnungen alter Meister in der Kunsthalle zu Bremen*, Frankfurt, 1916.
R.	Rovinski, *L'Œuvre gravé de Rembrandt*, St. Petersburg, 1895.
R. R.	Rovinski, *L'Œuvre gravé des élèves de Rembrandt et des maîtres qui ont gravé dans son goût*, St. Petersburg, 1894.
Schmidt.	Schmidt, *Handzeichnungen alter Meister*, Munich, 1884–1900.
Singer.	Singer, *Rembrandts Radierungen*, 3 folios.
Térey.	Térey, *Zeichnungen von Rembrandt im Budapester Museen*, Leipsic, 1909.
Valentiner.	Valentiner, *Die Handzeichnungen Rembrandts in Drei Bänden*, vol. I, Stuttgart, 1925.
V. D., Rembrandt.	Van Dyke, *Rembrandt and His School*, New York, 1923.
Weisbach.	Weisbach, *Rembrandt*, Berlin, 1926.

THE REMBRANDT
DRAWINGS AND ETCHINGS

THE REMBRANDT DRAWINGS
AND ETCHINGS

CHAPTER I

THE DRAWINGS

A COMPLETE list of the various drawings attributed to Rembrandt would probably number several thousand. The bulk of these drawings is so obviously not by Rembrandt, nor by any one of importance, that the more or less critical have agreed to reject fifty per cent of them. Doctor Hofstede de Groot has compiled a catalogue of over 1,600 drawings which he ascribes to Rembrandt, and the catalogue has been accepted by curators and collectors as the best extant.[1] But the De Groot list would seem in need of critical revision. It contains hundreds of drawings that are Rembrandtesque but are not by Rembrandt, some dozen or more that do not belong even in the school, and some further dozens that are of very questionable artistic value, no matter who did them. It is a snowball, like the aggregation of Rembrandt paintings, and has rolled up in it the more apparent drawings of the Rembrandt school, good, bad, and indifferent alike. Even the learned compiler himself offers doubts about certain items in his list.

I am told that when the fishing fleet arrives at Gloucester the catch is unloaded on the floors of the great warehouses and duly culled over by the dealers. Whatever can be named and is salable is taken out and put on the market; what is left over is called "floor stuff," and may be had almost for the asking. This seems to have been the method employed in selecting and assigning the Rembrandt drawings, not only by the various cataloguers, but by the curators in the European print-rooms. The best of the drawings have been given to Rembrandt, and what has been left over has gone to the pupils or followers of the school, or to the school generally. Every gallery or museum that has Rembrandt drawings has also one or two portfolios of "floor stuff" labelled "School of Rembrandt."

[1] Hofstede de Groot, *Die Handzeichnungen Rembrandts*, Haarlem, 1906.

1

It is usually a sorry collection. Connoisseurs keep turning it over and making guesses as to the authorship of certain drawings, but no one cares particularly about them, and, indeed, they are not worth caring about.

Even the drawings that are identified and given by name to pupils are so few, and often so feeble, that one wonders why this has not excited comment. To such well-known and capable pupils as Backer, Bol, Flinck, Eeckhout there are not given two dozen authentic drawings apiece, and to probably thirty or forty of the pupils not a scrap of any kind. I have not been able to find anything set down to the chief latter-day factotum of the school, Van der Pluym, nor anything unquestionable to Carel Fabritius or Drost or Horst or Victors or L. Van Beyeren or Levecq. The drawings assigned to such pupils as Lievens, Maes, and Hoogstraten, with few exceptions, merely provoke dissent by their poverty of numbers or their want of imagination or of skill. And they are usually not representative of their authors as Rembrandt pupils. For examples, the drawings assigned to Flinck and Lievens are late drawings, smacking of Van Dyck and Antwerp, and not of Rembrandt and Amsterdam, and the bulk of drawings given to Maes show him in his degenerate Netscheresque manner rather than in his Rembrandtesque manner.

What then happened to the drawings of the seventy or more known pupils and the score or more of unknown pupils or followers? Why should 1,600 (nearer 2,500) so-called Rembrandt drawings have survived and only a handful by all the pupils put together? Is it not possible that in the Rembrandt shop every good design by pupil or master was tossed into the shop portfolios and afterward sold in that bankrupt sale as Rembrandts? Is it not possible that scores of drawings that Rembrandt never saw have been handed down and sold under the Rembrandt name because that name would command a price? Is it not probable that the drawings repeat the story of the paintings, and that collectors, experts, and dealers have made the same snowball of the one as of the other? Indeed, in many instances the assignments of the drawings have closely followed those of the paintings. For instance, Bol's Tobias and the Angel, in the Louvre, and now under Rembrandt's name, was confirmed as a Rembrandt by finding Bol's tentative drawing for the picture. Both have been given to Rembrandt, and one has been made to prove the other, whereas both should have been given to Bol. No doubt the paintings led the way and the drawings followed after—the appropriation of the one calling for the further appropriation of the other. If there happened to be an etching of the same subject and composition, so much the better, for that made confirmation still stronger. In various ways—by mere blundering perhaps oftener than by direct intention—has the record been confused and art history made to tell the most remarkable cock-and-bull story ever handed down the centuries.

The inconsistencies of the story become more apparent as we go into the subject a little deeper. There are the drawings for Tobias and the Angel—ten of them. Why should any painter make ten drawings of one subject, and each one different from the other in models, composition, and method of handling? It is usual for a painter to make one or several drawings for a picture, but each is an addition or alteration or improvement on the other, and all of them are done in the same manner or method, and with the same kind of drawing. But ten! And all of them different one from another! The tale runs on. There are given to Rembrandt eight drawings of Isaac Blessing Jacob, seven of Manoah's Sacrifice, six of Jacob's Dream, twelve of Abraham Sending Away Hagar, nine of the Presentation in the Temple, nine of the Holy Family, six of the Adoration of Kings, six of the Adoration of Shepherds, eleven of the Good Samaritan. All this is, of course, put down to Rembrandt's indefatigable pains and patience in attaining perfection. But again almost every one of these drawings is different from the others in types, composition, and workmanship. Moreover, only a very few of them were ever worked up into pictures. Of the 1,600 or more accepted drawings in the *œuvre*, only about a score[1] can be identified as the drawings for paintings, and, as I maintain, even some of these are by pupils and not by Rembrandt.

And why in Protestant Holland all these drawings of religious subjects? The Reformation had practically banished church decoration, and there was no church demand for pictures in Rembrandt's Holland. But the religious theme was still carried on in the art schools. It was used in the Rembrandt shop and school to bring out the imagination, the invention, the skill in composition of the pupils. Biblical subjects were given out by Rembrandt to his pupils following the precedent of Lastman and Elsheimer. The good drawings by the pupils were probably not destroyed but kept in the shop portfolios, were used as occasion demanded, and were afterward sold at Rembrandt's bankrupt sale (knowingly or ignorantly, as you please) as Rembrandt's own work. The pictures and etchings by pupils were handled in the same way as the drawings—that is, sold from the shop or in the bankrupt sale with the Rembrandt name as trademark upon them. In no other way can one account for the medley of styles and manners running through the paintings, drawings, and etchings alike. There is no homogeneity about them.

[1] Doctor de Groot in his *Handzeichnungen Rembrandts* identifies a hundred more or less.

This lack of homogeneity is the most glaring inconsistency of all. The paintings, drawings, and etchings do not hold together as the work of one man, one individuality. A school likeness prevails throughout the bulk of them, but perhaps this is more apparent than real. Some works not of the school are included in the *œuvre*, together with many by incompetent hands. In the paintings one finds numerous portraits, in the etchings numerous beggars, and in the drawings numerous religious themes, but the models are, with some few exceptions, quite different in each, the compositions are seldom repeated, and the methods of handling are quite different again. The lack of consistency, the want of a pervading personality, are particularly marked in the drawings. The portfolios of many painters seem to have been mixed up or wrongly identified. Indeed, it almost looks as though different portfolios had gone in bulk to different museums and there been erroneously declared to be by Rembrandt. The collection of alleged Rembrandt drawings at Dresden is widely different from that at Berlin, and the drawings at Vienna vary widely again from those at Amsterdam. There is apparently only one way to deal with this entire mass of drawings, and that is to break it up into groups according to style, personality, and spirit. As the work of one man they are inconsistent and impossible. As the work of forty or fifty men they become, at once, plausible, and each group of drawings becomes homogeneous within itself and understandable as the work of some member (identified by name or otherwise) of the Rembrandt school.

In examining the original drawings in the European print-rooms the student will perhaps reach conclusions more readily, and with more certainty, than with the paintings, because the drawings have been less added to, less tampered with. In some cases later hands have made additions, perhaps with the object of making a picture out of the drawing and increasing its sale value. Sometimes the pen-and-ink drawings are reinforced in the foreground by some master correcting the pupil, or by the pupil himself. Again, a high light or a shadow is occasionally added, or a wash applied to give a tone effect. Then, too, there are a good many copies and some forgeries, but more often the drawings that look like copies of lost originals or forgeries are merely crude drawings by incompetent pupils, strangely mistaken for Rembrandt.[1] But I am not now directly concerned with detecting either copy or forgery as such. A copy or forgery that attempted

---

[1] "Wie kommt es, dass so zahlreiche Münchener Zeichnungen mit dem vollen Namen Rembrandts evident-falsch bezeichnet sind und die Zeichnung selbst mit demselben Material wie die Unterschrift: mit Kreide, spitzer oder breiter Feder, ausgeführt ist? Die Antwort kann doch nur so lauten: weil derjenige der die Unterschrift Rembrandts nachzuahmen suchte, auch selbst die Zeichnung gefälscht hatte." H. de Groot, *Die Handzeichnungen Rembrandts*, pp. 117–118.

to counterfeit the style of, say, Drost or Beyeren might be of value in suggesting a style now not too well understood.

Almost all of the drawings are in pen-and-ink, often rubbed in the shadows when wet by thumb or brush, or washed with sepia. There is a large number of drawings in red or black crayon with some of the crayon flaked off perhaps. Again there are drawings in pencil or silver-point, some upon tinted papers, and some done in water-colors. But the pen-and-ink sketches predominate. These latter are done easily and frankly as sketches, as studio memoranda, with never a thought of their being publicly exhibited or sold on the market.

It is inconceivable that such mere studio material should be signed by the designer, and yet many of the drawings bear the Rembrandt signature. It was probably attached at later dates, by collectors, for purposes of identification rather than deception. For examples, among the Rembrandt drawings in the Kaiser-Friedrich Museum one has the Rembrandt signature in German script, and with another the signature has been cut from some foreign document and pasted on the drawing. Also the name is varied in spelling in a way that could deceive no one, even if so intended. For examples again, some French collector, thinking of the name phonetically perhaps, attaches the signature "Rimbrant," and another writes down "Rimbaint." Almost always the signature is in a slightly different ink, and is a shade out of tone with the rest of the drawing, which would not be the condition were it attached by the draftsman himself at the time the drawing was made.[1]

There are, of course, cases where the signature, or autographic writing, was attached for the deliberate purpose of deception—cases where drawings by pupils have been put forth as by the master to deceive some dealer, collector, or amateur. But more often it is a case of misapprehension or mistaken identity. There is a red-chalk drawing in Berlin of Susanna and the Elders put down to Rembrandt. The drawing is by Lastman, and the picture after it, by Lastman, now hangs in the Kaiser-Friedrich Museum. But the drawing has on the back of it a memorandum about the prices of pictures, and this memorandum is thought to be in Rembrandt's handwriting; *ergo*, Rembrandt did the drawing on the face, as a copy of and following Lastman's picture! (Plate XLVII, 190.)

That seems a strange conclusion. Suppose Rembrandt were looking for a scrap of paper to make a memorandum upon, suppose he dipped

---

[1] "Nicht selten werden jetzt von gewissenlosen Händlern Signaturen darauf gesetzt, um ihnen in den Augen eines arglosen Sammlers den Stempel der Echtheit zu geben. Während also echte Bezeichungen auf Handzeichnungen Rembrandts zu den grössten Seltenheiten gehören, kommen unechte auch auf sonst einwandsfreien Zeichnungen sehr häufig vor." De Groot, *Die Handzeichnungen Rembrandts*, pp. ix–x.

into a portfolio of sketches for that purpose, why should he not have caught up a Lastman sketch as readily as one of his own? There would be nothing odd or unusual about his having a drawing by his master (Lastman) in his portfolio. In fact, a portfolio of Lastman's was sold in the Rembrandt bankrupt sale.[1] And he could not have cared a great deal about this one, for, like many of Lastman's drawings and paintings, it is as stiff and stake-like as a box of matches. But it is insisted by certain authorities that Rembrandt did the drawing. He loved the Susanna picture of his master and made the drawing from the painting. Well, then, why, if he were making a copy, did he not follow the model and make an *exact* copy? Why did he slightly change the position of the elders and nullify the background? Such a variation is not usual in a copyist, but it is usual with the master himself. The painter in his picture almost always departs from his sketch in certain features, and thus improves upon the original design. And these very variations have been used by experts hundreds of times to prove the genuineness of both drawing and painting. But here is a case where the rule proved something not wanted. What was wanted was the establishment of another Rembrandt drawing, and the rule was, for the moment, thrown out of the window.

Now if all this subtle reasoning to a premeditated conclusion is swept aside and the drawing is examined on its purely artistic record, it will be found to agree exactly with Lastman's formal, conventional, rather rigid art, and just as positively it will not agree with anything of Rembrandt's. Among the 1,600 or more drawings put down to Rembrandt, there are only two or three (and they are Lastman's) that will agree with this Susanna and the Elders. That in itself would have given a disinterested critic pause. But of recent years the hunt for Rembrandts has become an absorbing passion, and the real quarry being now practically non-existent in the open, it is not surprising that the eager pack should often trail home a school piece.[2]

The celebrated Saskia drawing at Berlin (Plate XV, 57) is another example of misapprehension or overanxious reasoning, and belongs in the same category with the Lastman. It is a small half-length drawing of a handsome young Dutchwoman resting her head upon her hand and looking out at the spectator. It is done in silver-point, and beneath it is an inscription, supposed to be by Rembrandt, saying that this

---

[1] "Un petit cahier de croquis dessinés à la plume par Pierre Lastman. . . . Un petit cahier de croquis à la sanguine par Pierre Lastman." Ch. Blanc's translation of the Rembrandt Inventory.

[2] Precisely the same kind of a drawing done by Lastman for his picture of Paul and Barnabas Preaching is reproduced by Freise in his work on Lastman (Plate 12), but, oddly enough, this drawing appears not so acceptable to the authorities as a Rembrandt.

is Saskia, his wife, whom he married on June 8, 1633. But Rembrandt married Saskia June 10, 1634—a year and two days later. Is it possible that he could not, and did not, remember his wedding-day? Doctor Hofstede de Groot thinks that an impossibility and explains that the word "getroudt" really meant "engaged" rather than "married"—"verlobt," as he translates it into German. But "getroudt" means "married" in the half-dozen Dutch dictionaries at my command, and also in the seventeenth and eighteenth century Dutch church books in America, some of which are in my personal custody. It never had any other meaning among the Dutch in America, and I doubt that the Amsterdam Dutch used it differently, except by literary license, poetic or otherwise.

It is quite apparent just why Doctor de Groot strains this point in argument. He wants to prove the drawing is *by* Rembrandt and *of* Saskia. He affirms that the inscription is in Rembrandt's handwriting, and possibly it is, but it must have been added at a later date than the drawing; and, while it certifies to the identity of Saskia, it says naught about Rembrandt himself doing the drawing. The inscription would have been just as appropriate had Flinck or Bol made the drawing.

I have recently examined the original at Berlin in full sunlight, and, I hope, with an open mind, but I could come to but one conclusion. The drawing is in silver-point and said to be on vellum, but I could not verify this material. There are glittering spots upon it, especially about the mouth. The inscription is at the bottom of the paper and seems to be of a darker shade, with no glittering spots upon it anywhere. It appears to be in pencil and of a later origin. Doctor Jan Veth, who has written so sympathetically about Rembrandt, agrees in thinking the inscription is of later origin than the drawing, but considers the drawing a genuine Rembrandt. I wish I could concur in this latter opinion, for I should like to agree with some one, and no one in preference to Doctor Veth; but I think the drawing by Flinck, for reasons which I shall give hereafter in considering Flinck's work. It is probable that Flinck did the drawing, and took it to Rembrandt for an inscription. Had Rembrandt signed his name to the inscription, it would have intimated that he did the drawing also. Had he done the drawing itself, there would have been no need in his day for either inscription or signature.

But the point of my illustrations should not be overlooked. Signatures and inscriptions upon drawings should be regarded with suspicion, especially if they lead up to an apparent commercial or collective purpose. As I have suggested, it was not, and is not now, customary to sign or inscribe drawings, though occasionally perhaps a painter might give a drawing to an admiring friend and inscribe it as an act of friendship. Usually drawings were regarded merely as memoranda to be used in the shop, and were not put upon the market. The later commercial value of the Saskia drawing was greatly enhanced by the inscription upon it, and that enhancement was, no doubt, foreseen by the inscriber, who may have been Rembrandt himself writing upon his pupil's drawing, and attesting as to the identity of the model.

It should, however, be understood that the instances of false Rembrandt signatures or false inscriptions upon the drawings, or forgeries of the drawings themselves, are not so great in number that they need worry the student. Nor are the additions to or modifications by alien hands of the original drawings many or very important. To be sure, some of the drawings have been "improved," finished up for prospective buyers by the addition of foreground or background, or an extra figure, but these additions are easily detected, not only by the difference in the tone of the ink but by the drawing. The additions are carefully, timidly done, and lack the verve of the original draftsman. The Offerings of Cain and Abel, in the Kaiser-Friedrich Museum (Valentiner, *Die Handzeichnungen Rembrandts*, vol. I, Plate 2), is a good illustration of this.

Usually the changes that may appear in a drawing have been made by the original draftsman as an afterthought, or as a correction of the moment. The drawings by Rembrandt himself for the Jan Six portrait are examples of this. The lines are large, swift, rather felt out in the doing than thought out beforehand. He was not interested in making some pretty sketch, but in jotting down fugitive memoranda, and where the first hasty stroke did not carry out his intention, he did not rub it out but corrected it by overlying strokes. This is apparent also in his drawing for Jan Six Standing at the Window, of which there is a well-known etching. (Plate I.)

In spite of false signatures, forgeries, copies, changes, alterations, in spite of the yellowing of time, the fading of ink, and the rubbing of surface, the drawings remain much simpler documents to deal with than the paintings. The color element is eliminated, to be sure, but so, too, is the repainting by the restorer. We are much nearer to the skeleton in the drawing than in the painting. This would seem to simplify the matter of attributions and make assignments more certain, and so it would were it not for the confusion created by erroneous assignments already made. Everything has been mixed and muddled in the interest or by the ignorance of amateurs, dealers, experts, and collectors. Rembrandt has been confused with his pupils, and the pupils with each other. To this confusion writers have added distorted legend and fanciful story to show how Rembrandt did all things right and his pupils all things wrong, to suggest that he had more avatars than Vishnu, and could produce anything in any style by virtue of superhuman genius, that he set a new style and type and invention for each pupil, and that they all followed his dictation and shone only by his reflected glory. It is a remarkable story of artistic exaltation in the master and consequent debasement in the pupils—this story of Rembrandt and his school.

Now amidst this confusion of draftsmen and styles it is very difficult to establish a criterion of any one man's work. It is, for instance, more difficult to pick the Rembrandts out of the 2,000 drawings than the Bols or the Eeckhouts. A man with the mannerisms of Aert de Gelder is rather easily detected, but Rembrandt, so far as I can make out, had few, if any, mannerisms. He is so vastly simple that he is difficult to apprehend—paradoxical as that may sound. I should be delighted could I be sure of fifty drawings by him now extant. I am less delighted by the two dozen I can find for, say, Salomon Koninck. And when the whole *œuvre* is gone over, piece by piece, there remains a residue of several hundred drawings that cannot be put down to either a name or a number, and must for the present be regarded as the insoluble part of the puzzle. There is nothing to be gained by carrying beyond the point of reasonable probability—a truth that will become self-evident as we proceed in our inquiry.

CHAPTER II

THE ETCHINGS

THE etchings are a more complicated problem than the drawings. The pen-and-ink sketch is almost always the work of one hand, but the etching may have been designed by one hand, put upon the plate by another hand, and worked upon by half a dozen other hands. Many of the Rembrandt plates bear evidence of having been worked over by various etchers at various times, for probably no other purpose than to produce new or unique "states," to be sold to collectors of the unique.[1] To add to this mix-up of etchers some of the plates have been changed in their surface by the use of the roulette-wheel or other instrument for darkening the impression and producing a "tone effect." A well-known etcher has told me that there are instances among the Rembrandt prints where this toning process is so thin and superficial that in the print it has been flipped off the paper with the finger. But of this I have no personal knowledge.

It will be remembered that in Rembrandt's day etching was still a comparatively new method. It had not entirely emancipated itself from engraving. Though independent sketch work was done with the needle, etching was still thought of as a reproductive process—a substitute in a measure for the engraving. Plates could be etched, toned, retouched in dry-point, pulled by a printer or by the etcher himself, and reproduced in any variety of states. A work of art was thus brought out and widely distributed at a comparatively small cost, and yet with a profit to the artist.

Many workmen employed the new method. It is a mistake to suppose that the etcher in Rembrandt's day was always (what is called to-day) a painter-etcher, a man producing independent and individual work. He was more often an engraver-etcher, turning out reproductive work with

---

[1] Middleton says: "There is good reason for suspecting that many later states (of the etchings) were entirely unknown to the master . . . rebitten and reworked they have been, and still are made to furnish impressions only to deceive the student and entrap the unwary." *Catalogue of the Etched Work of Rembrandt*, p. 18.

"There is at times so great and so serious a discrepancy between certain parts of the technic of an impression that we are justified in assuming that he allowed, in the particular case quoted, the inferior hand of an assistant to complete the plate." *Ibid.*, p. 21.

"A certain inequality of the work of the first ten years, as if different hands had been employed upon it." Haden, *Catalogue of the Etched Work of Rembrandt*, p. 30.

"In this year (1633) there were done in Rembrandt's studio more etchings alone than would have occupied a professed engraver a year. If Rembrandt did them, how, we would ask, did he manage to do thirty-three known pictures and a number of signed drawings besides? The two large plates of the Descent from the Cross would alone have occupied six months of his time." *Ibid.*, p. 42.

the help, perhaps, of shop assistants. It is another and more common mistake to suppose that an etching after a picture was necessarily done by the painter of the picture. A painter of rank could hardly afford the time for reproductive work, and there were shop workers who could, perhaps, do it better. An illustration to the point is the etching of the little Good Samaritan (Hind, 101) following the picture in the Wallace Museum, London. I have endeavored to show in my book on the Rembrandt paintings that the painting of the little Good Samaritan is not by Rembrandt, but by Simon de Vlieger.[1] Whether my conclusion about De Vlieger is acceptable or not, there seems some unanimity of opinion among Rembrandt students that the painting is not by Rembrandt. The assigning of the etching of the same subject to Rembrandt was purely arbitrary, without a scrap of proof or reason to substantiate it, and based wholly on the assumption that he did the picture, and must have done the etching also. There is no indication of Rembrandt's hand in the etching. Neither is there any indication of Simon de Vlieger's hand in it. The etching was done in some etcher-engraver's shop as a reproduction of a popular picture—done in a small, niggled, shop way, sold widely, no doubt, on account of its subject, and changed a number of times in its states for the purpose of producing further and wider sales. The workmanship of it, if closely compared with the plates of either Rembrandt or Simon de Vlieger, will show a different handling and reveal its shop origin.

The shop etcher is a person to be reckoned with, for he and his fellows are responsible for most of the famous plates attributed to Rembrandt. By "famous plates" I mean those large and labored etchings turned out in the Rembrandt shop by pupils and shop assistants. To be specific (and at the same time horrific, perhaps, to the general reader), I may cite such celebrated etchings as the Hundred Guilder Print, the Three Trees, the Three Crosses, the Christ Before Pilate, and almost all of the portrait plates that were used for book frontispieces or other illustrative purposes. They were worked upon by several hands, at perhaps different times, and when they were finished, if they received any signature at all, it was the shop trademark of "Rembrandt." On the plates of other painters the name or the initials of the painter is often given as the designer, and the etcher-engraver's name is sometimes added as the man who etched or published or sold the print. But the Rembrandt plates are given the shop trademark only, or else they remain unsigned.[2]

[1] Van Dyke, *Rembrandt and His School*, pp. 11, 175.
[2] Both Seymour Haden and Dutuit have noted that by the laws of the Hague Guild pupils were forbidden, during the time of their apprenticeship, to sign their works under penalty of a fine. "Par acte constitutif de la Guilde des peintres de La Haye, il était défendu à un élève, pendant le temps de son apprentissage de signer

These shop etchers greatly confuse the task of the critic or historian who would assign plates to certain individuals. The work of half a dozen hands in the Rembrandt shop—one perhaps doing the ground, another the landscape, a third the figures or the robes, and so on—creates a puzzle in itself; but when this is further added to by the long survival of the so-called Rembrandt plates, by their passing into unscrupulous hands in the eighteenth and nineteenth centuries, by their being reworked and toned by modern etchers to produce new and attractive states, the puzzle becomes something of a nightmare. No one can say where one hand leaves off and another begins. To find Rembrandt's needle in such plates is akin to finding the traditional needle in the haystack. Even the finding of his bare design is achieved, perhaps, more by faith than by consecutive reasoning.

That Rembrandt had the shop and used his pupils as shop workers there is little reason to doubt. Sandrart, who knew him from 1637 to 1641, has made positive record of the fact that Rembrandt's many pupils paid him one hundred florins apiece annually, exclusive of his profits from their pictures and *engravings*, which, in addition to his personal gains, brought him in some 2,000 to 2,500 florins.[1] This literary testimony is worthy of credence because it is borne out by the testimony of the etchings themselves. The *œuvre*, as regards the etchings, is made up of many plates from many hands. The simpler plates, in which only one hand is apparent, vary one from the other in manner and in method. It is impossible to see the versatility of genius in this variation. No person in art history has ever worked with brush, pen, or needle in so many different ways as Rembrandt is supposed to have worked. But the limit of probability has

ses propres ouvrages." Dutuit, *L'Œuvre Complet de Rembrandt*, p. 19. This accounts for Rembrandt's pupils—Bol, for instance—having no signed work to their names while pupils or workers in the Rembrandt shop. Everything went out under the shop name. Some early etchings by Lievens are signed, but that merely proves the rule quoted above, for Lievens was not a pupil but a fellow worker with Rembrandt. He was a year younger, and Coppier's theory is that they worked together on plates and signed together a monogram signature—R–L.

[1] "... und seine Behausung in Amsterdam mit fast unzahlbaren fornehmen Kindern zur Instruction und Lehre erfüllet, deren jeder ihm jährlich in die 100 gulden bezahlt, ohne den Nutzen welchen er aus dieser seiner Lehrlinge Mahlwerken und Kupferstucken erhalten der sich auch in die 2 bis 2,500 Gulden baares Gelds belauffen, samt dem, was er durch seine eigne Hand-Arbeit erworben." Doctor C. Hofstede de Groot, *Die Urkunden über Rembrandt*, p. 394.

Haden quotes Houbraken as saying: "He divided the whole upper part of the house into cellules or small studios for the reception of pupils, who by this kind of segregation were to preserve their individuality." Haden argues that he started out this way in 1630 with a house of unreasonable dimensions for a man of twenty-three unless he had some ulterior object in view. This object, according to Haden, was to form a school. He then quotes Sandrart as follows: "His house was constantly full of pupils of good family, who paid him 100 florins annually without counting the advantage he derived from their painting *and engraving*, which amounted to 2,000 or 2,500 florins more." Haden then asks: "Where are those engravings by which Rembrandt profited so largely but which the Catalogues make no allowance for?" (p. 20).

"Il tirait grand parti de ses élèves dont le nombre étoit considérable; il leur faisoit payer fort cher l'instruction qu'il leur donnait, et il vendoit toutes leurs copies, qu'il retouchoit quelques fois. Sandrart assure que ce commerce seul lui valoit 2,500 florins chaque année." Bartsch, *Catalogue Raisonné*, vol. I, p. xxii.

been overstepped. There are too many definite personalities passing under his name—personalities that have been identified. And why should a style indicating a personality or individuality be placed upon Rembrandt when it fits, perhaps, Bol or Eeckhout or Lievens so much better? Exclude the commercial and collective factors, and the allocation of so many different styles to Rembrandt becomes an absurdity.

I may follow up this argument by calling attention to the fact that there are some scores of etchings put down to Rembrandt, and generally accepted as authentic, that have no style whatever—etchings that are wholly negligible, plates that are merely inartistic botches. It may be assumed that Rembrandt was a genius, since no one is supposed to deny it, and it may be further assumed that all geniuses are primarily good craftsmen. If Rembrandt knew how to draw, how did he happen to do, for instance, that dreadful Old Woman in a Cottage (Hind, 76) that is so guileless of drawing? How did he do such wretched plates as the Man in Fur Cap (Hind, 59)? What is the meaning of such rubbish as the plates reproduced in Hind, 61, 63, 64, 66, 67, and 68? These and a dozen other plates, quite as hopeless, are put down to the year 1631. But in 1628, three years before, Rembrandt is credited with doing such work as the Portrait of his Mother (Plate III, 9). This etching of his mother is thought to be his earliest etching. The Rembrandt authorities accept it as by him, and I think rightly so. It is quite a perfect etching after its kind, and shows its author at twenty-two a master etcher for his time. The plates for 1631, three years later, which I have enumerated, are by some juvenile bungler, and have no technical nor artistic quality whatever. How is it possible to overlook and accept such wide variations in style, in method, in view-point? The inconsistency is too great.[1] Many plates have been rejected by the cataloguers and critics of Rembrandt because of their mediocrity, but several scores still remain in the *œuvre* that merit rejection—etchings that are too bad for the *œuvre*, not to mention Rembrandt the individual.

The presence of so many crude etchings in the *œuvre* makes quite understandable Joseph Pennell's contention that Whistler was a better etcher than Rembrandt. If Rembrandt did all the dull heavy work put down to him, he can hardly be placed in the front rank of etchers. And in still another respect Mr. Pennell was right. Neither Rembrandt, nor any one of his school or period, understood the possibilities and resources of etching so completely as such moderns as Whistler, Meryon, Buhot, without men-

[1] "How comes it that one etching, say of 1633, is so unlike and inferior to another etching of 1633 that one of them on the face of it is the work of the *master*, the other of the *man?*" Haden, p. 19.

tioning a dozen living etchers. The subtleties of line, the delicacies of tone, the contrasts of light and dark, the exact truth of values, the effects of half-tone, air, and envelope, and the methods of printing are all much better understood and employed with greater knowledge to-day than in the seventeenth century.

That merely argues growth in knowledge of the medium since Rembrandt's day, and in no way militates against Rembrandt. For his time he was quite a perfect etcher, and the Portrait of His Mother (Plate III, 9) which I have cited is, for pure line-etching, a complete performance. Whistler, in such a well-known etching as the Portrait of Dugros, handles his line perhaps with greater cunning, more delicacy, more play and flow of ink, but then perhaps he loses in Rembrandt's astounding simplicity and strength of characterization. At any rate, the differences do not put Rembrandt out of the running. Again, in the matter of envelope one must regard such celebrated etchings as the Hundred Guilder Print or the Three Crosses as rather tentative and experimental as compared with the full-length portrait of Annie Haden. The Whistler is much too modern for any etcher of Rembrandt's day. And yet the fact remains that Rembrandt was a great etcher—the greatest of his time, which is the most and best that can be said for any artist of any time.

The number of etchings put down as by Rembrandt has varied somewhat in the course of years. The early compilers had not too much critical insight and listed everything that was at all Rembrandtesque. As stated in my first Rembrandt book, Gersaint catalogued 341, Bartsch 375, Wilson 369, Dutuit 363, Blanc 356, Middleton 329, Sträter 280, Michel 270, Seidlitz 260. Almost all of these lists merely follow tradition and precedent. Criticism of the right kind, based on a study and knowledge of the technique of etching, was not seriously taken up until the time of Seymour Haden and Legros, both of them practical etchers. These men, knowing their material and their craft, were well qualified to pass on the technical merits or demerits of the Rembrandt prints, and they did so, with the result that Legros listed only 71 etchings, and, if I remember rightly, Haden even fewer.

But there is still an indisposition to accept the negations of Legros and Haden. Singer and Hind revert to the earlier lists, though Singer allows only about 140 plates. The Hind catalogue (1912, with a later edition, 1923) contains "a complete series of reproductions of the etchings" in 303 numbers. It is true, he accepts some of the etchings with reservations, some he rejects, and others he explains or apologizes for. But in the main he regards his list as accurate, and the etchings in it, in part at least, as belonging to Rembrandt's self. Upon what basis, other than the general resemblance running through all the work of the Rembrandt school, I am at loss to understand. It must be apparent to him that there are many different manners, many different hands visible in the plates. He continually notes that the plates have been "reworked" in the different states; he knows that many of them are mere shop etchings; that many, again, are unworthy of any etcher of rank. And he writes: "Admitting that the presence of a plate in Gersaint is a recommendation, it cannot rank as evidence in the face of the criterion of artistic quality." [1] Yet in the final accounting he leaves most of the etchings on Rembrandt's doorstep, because of a possibility that Rembrandt may have had something to do with them—Rembrandt the greatest etcher and painter of his day, and, all told, the most amazingly competent technician in art history!

And then, once more, as with the paintings and the drawings, the survival of hundreds of etchings with Rembrandt and practically none with his many pupils and followers! A few plates to Bol, a score to Lievens, and some of them doubtfully his, another score to Van Vliet, some "floor stuff" to Flinck, and some *disjecta membra* to Eeckhout and Koninck! Not a single plate to Van der Pluym, the wheel-horse of the Rembrandt coach, who was perhaps responsible for more of the Rembrandt shop etchings than Rembrandt himself; not a single plate to Horst, Drost, Bernaert, and Carel Fabritius, and forty other pupils! This is rather amazing when one considers again Sandrart's positive statement that Rembrandt's profits from the sale of his pupils' pictures and engravings (*kupferstücken;* literally, copper plates) brought him in some 2,000 to 2,500 florins a year. Perhaps the Rembrandt authorities will say that the pupils left so few plates because they were not etchers; but has not the same argument been used to maintain that they left so few drawings because they were not draftsmen, and so few paintings because they were not painters? Such an explanation would fail to explain. The only explanation of Rembrandt's survival in such large numbers of pictures, drawings, and etchings, and the corresponding non-survival of his pupils because of their limited number of pictures, drawings, and etchings, must be found in a planetesimal theory. The smaller bodies have been drawn into the greater. Only a few stray asteroids are now left spinning in outer orbits. The gravity, the drawing power of a great name, or a great price, has been irresistible.

As for the average survival of an old master's pictures after three hundred years, I endeavored to show in the *Burlington Magazine* (June, 1924)

[1] Hind, *Rembrandt's Etchings*, London, 1912.

that the figures for Dutch painters and their pictures given by Doctor Hofstede de Groot are too high.   He gives to Maes 570, Gelder 306, Bramer 355, Dou 390, Ovens 422, Jan Steen 890, Cuyp 840, Adriaen van Ostade 920, Wouvermans 1,160, Jacob Ruysdael 1,075.   The argument from this is that 700 for Rembrandt is not wide of the mark.   I now give the number of surviving pictures among the great Italians—those of Rembrandt's rank or approaching it—taking the lists as made up by Berenson.   He gives to Andrea del Sarto 42 pictures and frescoes, Fra Bartolommeo 51 and frescoes, Botticelli 35 and frescoes, Ghirlandajo 20 and frescoes, Leonardo da Vinci 8, Michelangelo 2 and the Sistine ceiling, Correggio 42 and frescoes, Cosimo Tura 33, Perugino 110 and frescoes, Raphael 53 and frescoes, Signorelli 56 and frescoes, Giovanni Bellini 43, Gentile Bellini 15, Carpaccio 47, Paris Bordone 64, Giorgione 17, Palma il Vecchio 54, Sebastiano del Piombo 36, Paolo Veronese 47, Titian 156, Tintoretto 183.   The greatest survival, it will be noticed, is with Tintoretto, known as the fastest workman of the Renaissance, and Titian, who lived to be ninety-nine, and worked up to a few months of his death.

I place these figures for the Italians beside those for the Dutchmen and submit that, on the score of probability alone, my figure of 48 pictures for Rembrandt (given in my book on the Rembrandt paintings) is nearer the mark than Doctor Bode's 550, or Doctor Valentiner's 800 odd.   And I submit, further, that the difference between the figures for the Dutchmen and the figures for the Italians is not to be accounted for by climate, or work, or time, but is due to the fact that the Italian lists have been prepared critically and the Dutch lists have not.   Dutch painting has never had a Cavalcaselle, a Morelli, a Venturi, a Berenson; it has had a Bredius, a Bode, a Hofstede de Groot, a Valentiner.   And as a result of indiscriminate determination every picture that by any stretch of the imagination could be given to Rembrandt has been added to the *œuvre*.

And now comes the same indiscriminate assignment of some 300 etchings and over 1,600 drawings to Rembrandt—practically more drawings than by all the great Italians I have named put together.   And again practically none by his seventy-two pupils.   I repeat, there is something wrong about this.   And as Mr. Roger Fry has said, apropos of this question: "The problem must be tackled.   We must come to some consensus of the best opinion on the question of Rembrandt's *œuvre*."

CHAPTER III

BASES OF ATTRIBUTION

MY method of inquiry regarding the Rembrandt drawings and etchings is substantially the same as that employed in considering the paintings. It is based in each case on a mental, emotional, and technical analysis of the work itself rather than upon tradition, documentation, or the say-so of experts. I do not despise or ignore the literary sources. Such works as Doctor Hofstede de Groot's *Rembrandt's Urkunden*—a compilation of Rembrandt documents—are very valuable, but they are, nevertheless, for the greater part transcripts of hearsay evidence, and have been so confused, contradicted, and denied that many of them are not acceptable as testimony. On the contrary, the work of art itself, painting, drawing, or etching, is first-hand, *prima-facie* evidence however much it may be distorted by additions or subtractions. I do not wish to imply a rejection of documentation, but rather a subordination of it to the work itself.[1]

There is, or should be, no change in a painter's mental, emotional, or technical attitude because he handles a pen or an etcher's needle instead of a brush. He varies and adapts his method to the material and the medium, but there is no marked shift in his point of view, his feeling, or his skill. If he can draw with the brush, he can do so with the pen or needle, and to put down an unintelligent, forceless sketch to a great man and apologize for it as "merely a sketch," is without reason or justification. A drawing may be ever so slight, but if by a master hand it will usually be quite right as far as it is carried. It may be hasty, not altogether ac-

[1] I shall put aside documentary and legendary evidence herein except as it may contribute, pro or con, to the evidence of the drawing or etching itself. That a drawing came from the Rembrandt bankrupt sale, or appears in an old dealer's catalogue, or is mentioned by some John Smith of the period, or was sold from some ducal collection, is not sufficient evidence of its authenticity. Every one knows the tales told about works of art by interested parties. Every art critic or expert of to-day receives weekly, if not daily, letters describing some old master in the writer's possession. It has always been in his family for at least a hundred years; it formerly belonged to the King of Spain or the Duke of Westminster, or Sir Thomas Lawrence, the painter painted it for Lorenzo de' Medici or the Prince of Holland, or at the least some great "swell," it has been expertized at the Hôtel Drouot or Christie's, or by some German professor; it is a great masterpiece and worth untold thousands. Will the critic be good enough to look at it? Well, occasionally the critic does look at it, and with the same result in almost every instance. The picture belies the description. In nine cases out of ten it is commercially and artistically worthless. And yet just such descriptions are accepted at their face values by the Rembrandt historians and cataloguers. We are told this Rembrandt drawing was done for Jan Six, and another drawing has Rembrandt's handwriting upon it, and still another was done for a book illustration; but when we see the drawings themselves they appear each different from the other, by a different hand, and not one of them by Rembrandt's hand. The literary records of the Rembrandt pictures, drawings, and etchings are too contradictory for acceptance by themselves considered.

curate, in need of changes and emendations; but the haste, the inaccuracy, the changes of a Rembrandt, or even a Lievens or a Bol, are not those of a beginner or a blunderer.   There may be a *cachet* of genius even in failure.

Nor does a change in the medium necessarily imply a change or variation of the theme employed.   Why should Rembrandt, who never did a beggar with the paint-brush, turn about and do fifty of them with the etching-needle?   Is there anything about a beggar standing, walking, or sitting that is peculiarly fitted to the etching-plate and not to the canvas? Why should Rembrandt, who is alleged to have done a dozen mountain landscapes with the paint-brush, not continue to do them with the etching-needle?   Do not mountain forms pile up on a copper plate as well as on a panel?   How does it happen that his alleged landscape etchings are all low-lying landscapes with scarcely a mountain among them?

Again, there is not among the paintings a single composition that is huddled in the grouping and lacking in space.   The early breadth and spaciousness of the Lesson in Anatomy runs on to the end in the Five Syndics, the Jewish Bride, the Family Group at Brunswick.   Even the Night Watch has space, and is far removed from any feeling of crowding, which is remarkable when it is considered that a certain number of portrait figures were ordered for that canvas, and had to go in, space or no space. On the contrary, consider in the etchings the continual massing and huddling of the figures.   Think of the Hundred Guilder Print, the Three Crosses, the Triumph of Mordecai, the Presentation in the Temple, the Christ Disputing with the Doctors, the Christ Before Pilate, all of them famous etchings, and all of them crowded with figures to the last degree. It would scarcely be possible to push additional figures into any of these plates.   Why did Rembrandt compose groups after that manner with the needle and not with the brush?

Still again consider the dramatic, not to say theatrical, quality in these etchings just mentioned, and then go back and parallel it with anything of the kind in the authentic paintings of Rembrandt, if you can.   The Syndics, the Jewish Bride, the Family Group at Brunswick, the Jan Six portrait, the Saskia and Coppenol at Cassel, the Christ and Magdalen at Brunswick are calm, grave, serene.   Even the Supper at Emmaus in the Louvre has a pause and a restraint about it.

Once more, why should a change in the theme and its form materially change an artist's mental and emotional individuality?   When Shakespeare passed from play to sonnet he did not alter his mental outlook with the acceptance of the sonnet form.   The sonnets are merely another phase of the same mind, the same genius.   It is true that the sketch is usually an unpremeditated affair—the first thought dashed down regardless perhaps of any final issue. And equally true that the etching may be an improvisation similar in result to the sketch, as witness the oft-referred-to etching of the Six Bridge (Plate XLII, 166). Any temperament may pass from grave to gay, from lively to severe, with a change of medium. But the painter of a Crucifixion to-day may be the etcher of a Kermess to-morrow without changing his quality or dropping his individuality. The subject or theme in art is of no great importance. A way of seeing and a manner of doing persists through any and all subjects. And the graveness of a Rembrandt could never pass into the buffoonery of a Steen or an Ostade.

Nor is it conceivable that a method of treatment peculiar to an artist's paintings should greatly change in his drawings or etchings. I mean merely that Rembrandt, who saw so largely and completely and handled so broadly even in his early Lesson in Anatomy, and continued to see and handle that way to the end of his career, would never do such a small, niggled etching as the Good Samaritan (Hind, 101), or the Raising of Lazarus (Hind, 96), or the Christ Before Pilate (Hind, 143). The artistic constitution of the man, his mental make-up, painter's vision, and craftsman's hand were all opposed to such minute seeing and doing. To turn a moment from negative to positive illustration, consider the painted portrait of Jan Six—perhaps the most complete and noble portrait expression in the whole realm of Dutch art. The mind, the vision, the hand here are all supremely broad and comprehensive. It is impossible to conceive of simpler form, or fewer brush-strokes, or more complete results. Would you expect for such a work a pretty and petty drawing such as Gerard Dou might put forth? Fortunately we have the Rembrandt drawing for this portrait. I reproduce it herein (Plate I, 2). There, in the first thought for the portrait, you have the very body and bones, the bulk of vision and handling, that I have been trying to describe. One supplements and complements the other. The same hand did both sketch and portrait. And there you have a positive and right view of Rembrandt as draftsman and painter. It is doubtful if he ever had any different manner of seeing or doing from this. It was his endowment by nature, and he could no more have changed it than a leopard could change his spots. And there was no need to change.

Now there is another drawing for Jan Six—the one in an interior with the figure standing at the window (Plate I, 4). It is done in precisely the same broad free way as the portrait sketch mentioned above, and is of similar quality. There is also an etching after this sketch, supposed to be done by Rembrandt in 1647 (Plate I, 3), but this etching bears an entirely different surface handling from the drawing. Examine it closely—under a glass if necessary—for its worried, fussed-over and niggled workmanship. Is it possible that Rembrandt of the broad hand, as shown in the two drawings and the Jan Six painted portrait, could have done this plate? Hardly. The plate is a shop affair, mauled and re-worked in the course of time by many hands. In spite of that, it is an imposing and amazing etching, but to attribute it to Rembrandt, save as he prepared the design, is shooting wide of the mark.

My argument naturally implies that artistic somersaults are turned more in the fancy of connoisseurs and collectors than by artists themselves. There is a consistency about every artist of note, a sameness of thinking and doing, that persists throughout his work from beginning to end. A well-known modern painter once said to me that every now and then he would start a fresh canvas with the determination to do something different from anything he had ever done before, but at the end of the week the result was "the same old thing." The story, I think, illustrates common experience, even with men of genius. Art history recites it on every page. A certain repetition is the expected thing, even to-day. A portrait is painted by Sargent or Lavery or Orpen with the distinct knowledge of every one concerned that it will be a Sargent, or a Lavery, or an Orpen—that is, like the other Sargents, Laverys, and Orpens. It was always so. No one ever sat to Titian, Velasquez, or Frans Hals with the idea that he would get a portrait that would look like a Raphael or a Murillo or a Van Dyck. The similarities and repetitions in a man's style are the features by which we are able to recognize his pictures. They are the chief bases of connoisseurship.[1]

The signature upon the etchings, as upon the paintings or drawings attributed to Rembrandt, is, of course, more or less suspect. On the drawings it may have been written in by latter-day owners to indicate merely their belief that Rembrandt did the drawings, and, lest posterity should forget or fail to recognize, they would write down the signature in good

---

[1] Middleton wrote years ago, in his *Catalogue of the Etched Work of Rembrandt* (p. 2), that "the most regardless observer must have remarked the singular variation, from time to time, in his [Rembrandt's] style and execution." Doctor de Groot and his following account for this wide variation in the style of the Rembrandt *œuvre* by saying he was a great genius and had many styles. If he had many styles, then he is the one great exception in the whole history of painting. But this is not believable. Rembrandt did not, could not, draw like a great master in one drawing and then, almost in the same breath, draw like a veritable tyro. He did not draw at sixty precisely and in the same way as at twenty, but he always drew like Rembrandt. He never drew like Bol or Lievens or Eeckhout or Maes. I have made herein a list of his drawings and etchings, as in my former volume a list of his paintings. No one disputes their authenticity. They are his masterworks and show him from youth to old age. There is no medley of styles about them. They show one distinct personality—one distinct mind, view-point, and hand. They should form a proper criterion for Rembrandt's style.

black ink. But with the etchings the name had to be cut in the plate, usually in reverse—quite a different matter, but not a difficult one. Any engraver could do it. , And since the plates endured and passed from hand to hand, some of them surviving to this day, cutting of the name could have been done at any time. In Rembrandt's day that name was little more than a trademark. It is no more than that at the present time as regards the etchings.

The appearance of the signature is somewhat capricious. The landscapes reproduced in Hind, 238, 239, and 265, are all by the same hand, but two of them are signed and one is not. Many plates are without the signature. And, as with the drawings and paintings, it takes various forms. Middleton speaks of "the varying forms of his signature," and says regarding the 350 plates assigned to Rembrandt that 152 have no name or date, 179 are undated, 142 are signed "Rembrandt," 62 with the monogram "RH," 3 with the letter R. And Seymour Haden writes: "The signature and date upon a plate might, with reason, be supposed to indicate the time of the execution. It does not necessarily do so. It is often not found upon it till the second or third state, or even, as in the case of the great Christ Before Pilate, till the sixth state of the plate. . . . Weeks, months, and even years may elapse between the printing of the first and the printing of the sixth state; and, after all, the date found on that plate may refer not to the time of its composition and first printing but to the sixth printing of it." (Page 17.) The ease with which it could be put on and the commercial value that would result from its use should be considered.

The signatures of pupils (after they had left the Rembrandt shop) upon etching-plates is another story. They are more believable as less sought for by collectors and less valuable in commerce. The signature of Van der Pluym or Drost on a plate would be credible because there would be no motive in its forgery—neither name being of much value to the collector or dealer. With well-known pupils like Bol, or a Rembrandt associate such as Lievens, there would be more temptation, and in a few cases perhaps these names have been wrongly signed. The money value of the signature is the determining factor. Suspicion may be aroused as this is great or small.

CHAPTER IV

REMBRANDT THE MASTER

I MUST, at the start, confess to difficulty in establishing a criterion for Rembrandt's drawings that shall be broad enough and inclusive of his entire work. For the paintings we have material to our purpose in pictures extending throughout his entire life, pictures that are his beyond dispute. But for the drawings we are vastly more limited, as will presently appear. By way of beginning we may start with one drawing—that for the Jan Six portrait—which will give us a method and a medium perhaps employed by Rembrandt late in his career.

The chief Jan Six drawing (there are more than one, as I shall indicate in the lists that follow) is in the Six collection, at Amsterdam. It is in black chalk or coal, and on its face attests its genuineness. It is reproduced herein beside the oil portrait, to show the simplifying process undergone in the painting (Plate I, 2). The first thought in the drawing was largely concerned with the costume, the broken lines, catches of light, masses of shadow, but when Rembrandt came to paint the picture he pushed all the smaller work aside and put in the whole portrait in broad masses and flat brushing. This change in itself rather confirms the belief that the drawing was done *before*, and not *after*, the painting. If the drawing were done *after* the portrait, done by a pupil, follower, or forger, it would hardly have been varied in the drawing, at the least not by adding detail that was detrimental to it. Besides, the freedom of the drawing, its firmness and sureness, belong to a hand that was not following, but leading. The hand was blocking out large areas and indicating the planes with confident knowledge. There can be little if any doubt that Rembrandt did the drawing, especially as we find it confirmed in every way by the drawings for the Jan Six at the Window and the Five Syndics. They confirm one another and must be accepted as Rembrandt's work with the crayon at a certain period of his career, say about 1650 or a little later.

This is a simple deduction, a conclusion easily arrived at. But what about Rembrandt's drawing at other periods? Was he always so very simple and so very broad? When younger did he do things in a more minute and careful way? And what about his drawing in other mediums than black chalk? If he worked in pen-and-ink the line would probably be finer than in crayon. Did he use wash to gain breadth or tone?

Did he work in silver-point or red chalk or water-color? We now enter upon uncertain ground and must move cautiously. It would seem the better plan to work backward from the Jan Six drawings to the earlier styles, employing such antennæ as we may possess to feel out not only his technical methods in their variations but the Rembrandt subjects through his mental and emotional attitudes toward them. This is not easily done in black-and-white drawings. The absence of color limits not only his expression but our perception. It is necessary to move carefully and not allow any *flair* of feeling that such and such a drawing is "unmistakably Rembrandt" to stampede us. A scientific inquirer should be anxious to discern and establish the different manners of Rembrandt in as many drawings as possible, but he should be more anxious not to commit any grave blunder of acceptance.

I have already intimated that it is easier to locate the drawings of the more mannered painters such as Bol, Koninck, or Aert de Gelder than those of a great genius like Rembrandt. His very simplicity, his scorn of small expedients, his carelessness in making pictorial memoranda, may entirely mislead us. Therefore, in method of procedure perhaps it would be the safer way at the start to take out of the 1,600 or 1,700 drawings attributed to him the ones that are not by him, and then consider the remainder. It is perfectly possible to eliminate several hundred of these drawings as being too crude and unintelligent for him, several hundred that are opposed to his style as shown in his paintings, several hundred more that can, with confidence, be given to his pupils and followers, and still several hundred that are not even Rembrandtesque, or are of no artistic value whatever.

This I have done, and from the remainder tried to make up a list of the Rembrandt drawings. But, it must be confessed again, with disappointing results. The process of elimination still leaves me with no more than a shadowy criterion for the earlier work—the formative period. Again and again I have supposed a case, assumed a premise and a style, and conducted a test, but found no solution. I regret that the count of drawings that I have been able to make up is so meagre, and yet I recognize that its very meagreness rather bears out the conclusion expressed in my book on the paintings, that Rembrandt was a portrait-painter, and did little beyond portraits.

Do portrait-painters always make sketches or drawings of their sitters? Rembrandt did make portrait sketches in several instances that have been under consideration, but were not these perhaps exceptional? What of the sketches for his other portraits? Did these ever exist? Figure and subject painters, of course, do, as a rule, make preliminary sketches for their work; but Rembrandt, according to our findings, did not concern himself to any great extent with historical painting. He made his reputation with portraiture, and it is doubtful if he went much beyond that. It is even doubtful that he was a great producer in any department, either in painting or etching. He was a *chef d'école*, the master, the proprietor of a great art shop, a person who planned and directed and taught, who bought and sold pictures and etchings, other painters' work as well as his own, and who, perhaps, painted and etched only for great patrons with important commissions.

The Rembrandt etchings have undergone with me the same process of investigation as the drawings, and determinations have been made on similar grounds and for similar reasons. The same doubts, the same uncertainties are here as there. If one could be absolutely sure of, say, half a dozen etchings we should then have, in some measure, Rembrandt's method of handling the needle.[1] But almost everything has to be arrived at by circumstantial evidence, by hypotheses, by feeling in the dark. His shop work is so much easier recognized. Its very worried and tortured look discloses its identity. These shop etchings I have listed by themselves. The larger part of the etchings given to Rembrandt himself is listed tentatively, and is by no means a complete list. There is confusion now, and there doubtless was in Rembrandt's day, and in his own shop, over what was his and what that of his pupils or shop workers. In the early etchings I find Rembrandt and Lievens almost inseparable, and am forced to the conclusion that, being friends and fellow pupils, they perhaps worked together on the same plates, in the same or a similar manner. This conclusion is also that of Coppier, whose book[2] puts forth the theory of joint workmanship and a joint signature—R–L.

It is true that we have some etchings by Lievens that would seem to indicate his individual method of work, but all of the Lievens plates now extant were done after he left Amsterdam and Rembrandt and had taken up residence in Antwerp. They are in his Antwerp manner; most of them were put out and signed by Wyngaerde, an Antwerp print dealer, and perhaps worked by him, which starts one groping once more for Lievens's peculiar way of working. When he and Bol and Van der Pluym were (at different periods) Rembrandt's shop assistants, who knows what plates they did that were possibly inspired or retouched by Rembrandt? A shop product was being turned out and sold on the market, and perhaps at that

---

[1] "The earlier prints, however beautiful, are apparently utterly unlike the prints of his later days; so unlike that one might almost fancy that we were viewing the productions of a different hand." Middleton, p. 5.

[2] Coppier, *Les Eaux Fortes de Rembrandt*, Paris, 1922.

time no one cared very much who did this part or that. The product was a blend, a fusion—the same fusion that later on, with many hands and many additions, passed into a confusion.

Amid this uncertainty we shall be able to point out the designer more certainly than the etcher. It is, for example, quite apparent that the large Christ Before Pilate was designed by Salomon Koninck. It has his ear-marks in composition, types, studio costumes, materials, and agrees perfectly with the Pilate Washing His Hands in the Metropolitan Museum. This Metropolitan picture and the Christ Before Pilate in the National Gallery, London, are given erroneously, as I think, to Rembrandt. And so also is this etching. All three of them belong to Koninck. But Koninck himself did not do the work on the etching-plate. It is shop work —either his shop or Rembrandt's, I know not which. Several hands have worked over the surface. This is the story of many of the so-called Rembrandt etchings. Who etched them it is difficult to say.

As for the landscapes, in both etchings and drawings, given to Rembrandt, I cannot trace his hand in them with any certainty. They have been assigned to him apparently without warrant. Seymour Haden gave an opinion to that effect which should have been accepted. They seem to have been done by half a dozen hands. Some of them are very good, but perhaps not so wonderful as we have been assured. Mr. Pennell and Mr. Hind tell me that the Gold Weigher's Field (Plate XLI, 164) is quite perfect, and I am glad to agree in measure, but the use of the superlative seems hardly warranted. The same hand did the less satisfactory Amsterdam (Plate XLI, 163), but it was not Rembrandt's hand. I do not know who did them. Collectors and dealers insist upon the great glory of the Three Trees (Plate XLVI, 184), but it is a plate botched in the foreground and sky, and now of good report only in the background. An unpretentious plate such as the Landscape with Trees (Plate XLIV, 174), which Mr. Hind has the good taste to admire, is worth a dozen of the Three Trees. With a few exceptions I am not able to name the authors of the so-called Rembrandt landscape etchings. I have listed many of them hereafter under the work of Unknown Pupils and Followers, placing them in kindred groups, and giving them letters or numbers. To Rembrandt himself I have ventured to assign tentatively a few landscape drawings that seem to be in his style.

CHAPTER V

DRAWINGS AND ETCHINGS BY REMBRANDT

THE following lists of drawings and etchings belonging to Rembrandt are by no means final or complete. No doubt Rembrandt had a hand in many sketches and plates that I have not been able to recognize because lacking in outstanding characteristics. The lists here made up are based almost wholly upon distinctions and characteristics. The aim is to discriminate between the different styles and manners shown in the Rembrandt *œuvre*, to set apart Rembrandt from his pupils, to establish the artistic identity of the pupils, to point out the differences, for example, between Rembrandt and his fellow worker Lievens, between Flinck, Bol, and Eeckhout; and, further, to establish the differences by reference to drawings and etchings correlated and brought together in distinctive groups, each group disclosing a positive individuality.

In establishing a group for Rembrandt I shall content myself with a sufficient number of drawings and etchings to indicate a style. I am aware that the limited number of works I assign to him puts definite limitations upon his versatility. I do not find that he could do any and all things in any and all ways. Such an idea of him has been established by the acceptance of any and all the works in the *œuvre* as by his own hand. That seems to me impossible—a false idea. At any rate the drawings and etchings I have given to him show him as a draftsman and etcher from the beginning to the end of his career, and they are all of a kind in manner of seeing and doing. They are distinctly characteristic and positively individual.

DRAWINGS BY REMBRANDT

AMSTERDAM:
RYKS MUSEUM

MAN SEATED
Lilienfeld, Amsterdam, 24.

This drawing has been identified as a study for the man at left in the Rembrandt picture of the Five Syndics at Amsterdam. The identification is not absolute, though the drawing is apparently by Rembrandt. It is a washed and toned drawing, and in that respect a little unusual with Rembrandt, but there can be little question that he did it. With a remarkable effect of light.

AMSTERDAM:
SIX
COLLECTION

*PORTRAIT OF JAN SIX
Hind, D., Pl. XII; Neumann, 41.

Described in the text to this volume. (Page 19.) One of the most satisfactory of all the Rembrandt drawings. A comparison with the painting, reproduced herewith, will indicate the simplifying process undergone in the painting. Another version in Warwick Collection, and another in the Louvre, Paris.

*JAN SIX STANDING AT WINDOW
Hind, D., XXV.

A drawing done hastily, no doubt, as a mere notation for the etching. It has been amended, by Rembrandt himself, in the lower part of the figure, the dog, and elsewhere.

JAN SIX STANDING AT WINDOW
Hind, D., XXVI.

A transfer drawing of the above, made for the etching, probably by a shop assistant.

SKETCH FOR DEYMAN ANATOMY LESSON
Neumann, 43.

AMSTERDAM:
BEETS
COLLECTION

PRESENTATION IN TEMPLE
Valentiner, vol. I, 319.

A blurred and vague memorandum, perhaps by Rembrandt.

AMSTERDAM:
JANSEN
COLLECTION

REMBRANDT IN PAINTING CLOTHES
Neumann, 38; Heseltine, 1.

A very strong drawing, giving the sturdy character of the figure with few but effective lines. The angular, almost square cubist quality of the drawing (notice the feet) is remarkable. This drawing was formerly in the Heseltine Collection.

THE WIDOWER
Heseltine, 18; Hind, D., XXXIII.

In Rembrandt's style but possibly not by him. It is perhaps nearer to Nicolaes Maes. Assignment tentative and given here more for contrast with the Rembrandt in Painting Clothes than for entire agreement.

BERLIN:
KAISER-
FRIEDRICH
MUSEUM

STUDY FOR THREE OF THE SYNDICS AT AMSTERDAM
Lilienfeld, Berlin, 91.

The drawing not entirely intact. Probably there was more to it when originally done. Scrubbed a bit for light effect. Merely a Rembrandt notation of a first impression.

*VIEW OF LONDON
Lilienfeld, Berlin, 161; Hind, D., XXI.

This is one of the few drawings of landscape that seems to suggest Rembrandt's mental grip and technical force. It is probably his work,

* The asterisk indicates that the etching or drawing is reproduced in this volume.

though several landscape-painters among Rembrandt's contemporaries might, with some reason, be credited with it.   Unfortunately we have no absolute criterion in landscape for Rembrandt, though there are plenty of landscapes superficially resembling this one that have been assigned to him.   It has the Rembrandt firmness, and is a superb drawing.   Another and more detailed drawing of the same subject at the Albertina, Vienna.   De Groot thinks it a copy, but Hind does not agree.

A Jew
Lippmann, Fourth Series, 35.
> Attribution tentative.

Blind Belisaurus
Lilienfeld, Berlin, 86.
> Merely a hasty memorandum.

Landscape
Lilienfeld, Berlin, 160; Hind, D., XX.
> Done with silver-point and finer than the wash and ink of the London Landscape (Lilienfeld, Berlin, 161), but the same hand is at work.   It is probably by Rembrandt.   Compare with Terey, Budapest, 25, 26, and Bol, following Rembrandt but weaker, in Michel, vol. 2, page 62.

The Levite's Concubine
Valentiner, vol. I, 144.
> Listed tentatively.   An excellent drawing.

BUDAPEST
MUSEUM

*Landscape with House
Terey, Budapest, 25; Meder, 549.

Landscape with House
Terey, Budapest, 26; Meder, 549.
> Both of these Budapest landscapes seem in the style of the London Landscape (Lilienfeld, Berlin, 161) and the silver-point landscape at Berlin (Hind, D., XX), and both are excellent.

Portrait of Coppenol
Terey, Budapest, 5.
> In a style afterward followed by Horst.   Probably by Rembrandt. At any rate a forceful drawing.

DRESDEN
MUSEUM

Christ Preaching
Lilienfeld, Dresden, 22.
> Another hasty memorandum, confused in the grouping.

Return of the Prodigal
Valentiner, vol. I, 391; Lilienfeld, Dresden, 24.
> A very good drawing and quite worthy of Rembrandt.   It is less amended and more certain in the first stroke than many of his draw-

1. REMBRANDT: PAINTING OF JAN SIX
Six Collection, Amsterdam

2. REMBRANDT: DRAWING OF JAN SIX
Six Collection, Amsterdam

3. REMBRANDT: ETCHING OF JAN SIX AT WINDOW
H. 228

4. REMBRANDT: DRAWING OF JAN SIX AT WINDOW
Six Collection, Amsterdam

PLATE I

5. REMBRANDT: DRAWING OF LADY WITH FAN
British Museum, London

6. REMBRANDT: DRAWING OF YOUNG MAN
HOLDING FLOWER
Louvre, Paris

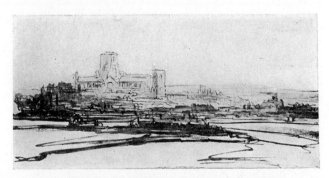

7. REMBRANDT: DRAWING OF VIEW OF LONDON
Berlin Museum

8. REMBRANDT: DRAWING OF LANDSCAPE WITH HOUSE
Budapest Museum

PLATE II

9. REMBRANDT: ETCHING OF PAINTER'S MOTHER
H. 1

10. REMBRANDT: ETCHING OF THE PAINTER IN SOFT CAP
H. 57

11. REMBRANDT: ETCHING OF EPHRAIM BONUS
H. 226

12. REMBRANDT: ETCHING OF ARNOLD THOLINX
H. 289*

PLATE III

ings. Nicolaes Maes afterward adopted this style, following Rembrandt.

RESURRECTION OF TABITHA
Neumann, 79; Lilienfeld, Dresden, 35.

DEPARTURE FOR HUNT
Lilienfeld, Dresden, 67.

PEASANT COTTAGE AND TREES
Lilienfeld, Dresden, 94.
> In the style of the Budapest landscapes listed above.

DRESDEN:
FRIEDRICH
AUGUST II
COLLECTION

OLD MAN AT TABLE
Lilienfeld, Dresden, 113.

HAARLEM:
TEYLER
MUSEUM

FOUR FIGURES
No. 0 52.
> Not entirely convincing as a Rembrandt.

CHRIST WITH DISCIPLES
No. 0 47.
> Attribution tentative.

TWO MEN
N. N.
> It is probably by Rembrandt.

THE HAGUE:
HOFSTEDE DE
GROOT
COLLECTION

CHRIST HEALING A LEPER
Valentiner, vol. I, 412.
> I have not seen the original drawing and judge it only in reproduction. Assignment tentative.

DANIEL IN LION'S DEN
Neumann, 21; Valentiner, vol. I, 210.
> Assignment tentative. The drawing excellent, but not entirely convincing as a Rembrandt.

HAMBURG:
KUNSTHALLE

STUDY FOR ST. JEROME
Lippmann, Third Series, 133.
> This is the study for the etching of St. Jerome Reading in an Italian Landscape (Hind, 267). It was probably done by Rembrandt, and the etching worked up in the shop from the drawing.

LAUSANNE:
STRÖLIN
COLLECTION

NOAH'S ARK
Valentiner, vol. I, 6.
> In the Rembrandt manner, and very effective in its values and planes.

*LADY WITH FAN

Hind, B. M., 56; Bell, Pl. X.

This is a drawing for the Rembrandt Portrait of a Lady in the Ryks Museum. The painting I listed tentatively in my first volume under Lievens, saying that both Lievens and Rembrandt may have worked upon it, and I was unable to say what was Rembrandt's share of the work. The Lievens earmarks about it were perhaps given undue importance and Rembrandt's part minimized unwittingly. But there can be no doubt about Rembrandt having done the drawing. Perhaps he contented himself with that, and let Lievens work up the picture from his sketch. The sketch is supposed to have been done about 1639, but it will be noticed that its style is practically that of the Jan Six drawing done in 1654, fifteen years later. This does not prove that he worked in no other, no finer or more finished style, but it does indicate that he did not at any time do fingers and faces after the manner of Gerard Dou, or make drawings with graceful modulated lines like Lievens, or scratchy backgrounds like Koninck. Like all great men, he probably did things in one way because he had early decided that that way was the best way.

STUDY FOR THE ANSLO ETCHING

Hind, B. M., 59, p. 28.

A sketch for the etching (Hind, 187). The drawing is by Rembrandt but the etching has been done in the shop chiefly, I should say, by Bol, who was at this time, 1641, in the Rembrandt shop working as a helper. The background shadows of the etching have Bol's network, and the coat and table-cloth his cross-hatching.

SKETCH FOR THE SYLVIUS ETCHING

Hind, D., Pl. XXVII.

The sketch by Rembrandt does not positively show the shadowed hand on the frame, which appears in the etching. It may be that this was an interpolation in the shop where the etching was done by assistants.

CHILD BEING TAUGHT TO WALK

Hind, B. M., 81, p. 35.

There is a possibility of this drawing being by Rembrandt, and I list it tentatively.

MAN IN WIDE-BRIMMED HAT

Hind, B. M., 85, p. 36.

A superficial resemblance to Rembrandt drawing, but hardly sure enough in structure for the master. Assignment tentative.

WOMAN AT A WINDOW

Heseltine, 20; Lippmann, First Series, 92.

An excellent washed drawing, quite worthy of Rembrandt, and very much in his style. It must be accepted as by him for the present at least, though there is doubt about it. It is perhaps by Nicolaes Maes.

Town Hall of Amsterdam
Lippmann, First Series, 38.
>   Probably by Rembrandt.

The Farm
Heseltine, 24.

LONDON:
  HOLFORD
    COLLECTION

Portrait of Man in Chair
>   Rembrandt in part.

MUNICH:
  OLD
    PINACOTHEK

Study for Abraham Francken
>   A study for the etching, reproduced in Hind, 291.

OXFORD:
  UNIVERSITY
    GALLERIES

Christ and Woman of Samaria
Valentiner, vol. I, 403.
>   A drawing of a woman by an unknown pupil, probably corrected by Rembrandt with black chalk in the figure of Christ at right. An Annunciation at Berlin (Valentiner, vol. I, 288) also has a similar Rembrandt correction in the angel.

PARIS:
  LOUVRE

The Omval
Lippmann, Third Series, 18.
>   A drawing for the Omval etching (Hind, 210) listed hereafter and possibly by Rembrandt—the etching being worked upon in the shop.

Jan Six
No. 22919.
>   Another version of the Six drawing.

*Young Man Holding Flower
No. 22917; Neumann, Pl. 44.
>   Quite in the Rembrandt manner. Compare with the Jan Six drawings.

Two Landscapes
No. 22894.
>   Two landscapes on one sheet. The top one may possibly be by Rembrandt.

Portrait of Man
Lippmann, Third Series, 1.

Portrait of Man
Lippmann, Third Series, 2.
>   This is a drawing on the reverse of the No. 1 listed above. It is more sketchy than No. 1, but is probably of Rembrandt origin.

Portrait of Anslo
Lippmann, Third Series, 17.
>   It hardly lives up to Rembrandt, but is put down here tentatively for its possibilities. Another drawing of the same subject in British Museum, Hind, B. M., 59, p. 28.

PARIS:
  LOUVRE,
  BONNAT
  COLLECTION

STUDY OF A WILLOW
Hind, D., Pl. XXII.

An excellent study, perhaps a first sketch for the St. Jerome etching (Hind, 232), or perhaps used in connection with the Omval etching (Hind, 210).

PARIS:
  MATHEY
  COLLECTION

MILITARY MAN
Lippmann, Third Series, 32, H. de G., 800.

Attribution tentative.

PARIS:
  MOREAU-
  NÉLATON
  COLLECTION

ARTIST AT WORK
Lippmann, Fourth Series, 51.

ROTTERDAM:
  BOYMANS
  MUSEUM

ABRAHAM WITH THE ANGELS

A strong sketch but nevertheless put down to Rembrandt with a query. See the same subject under Aert de Gelder's etchings.

STOCKHOLM
  MUSEUM

HOMER DICTATING

Quite in the Rembrandt manner. Perhaps the drawing for the picture of Homer at The Hague.

CHRIST AND MAGDALEN
Kruse, II.

This is similar to the Brunswick picture as regards composition. It is, perhaps, a following of the picture. It is Rembrandt with a query.

VIENNA:
  ALBERTINA

SKETCH FROM RAPHAEL'S CASTIGLIONE
Hind, D., IV.

WARWICK
  CASTLE
  COLLECTION

JAN SIX
Michel, vol. II, p. 178.

Another version, perhaps a copy.

ETCHINGS BY REMBRANDT

BRITISH
  MUSEUM

*REMBRANDT'S MOTHER, 1628
Hind, 1.

If this be accepted as by Rembrandt, then it must be admitted that Rembrandt at twenty-two was an almost perfect etcher. The reproduction in Hind is not as good as in Singer, but the print in the Teyler Museum, Haarlem, should be seen. The drawing for pure line-etching is quite beyond cavil. After this performance at twenty-two the dreadful small heads and small beggars of 1630, 1631, 1632, are not admissible. Great artists do, of course, vary in accomplishment, but not to the extent here indicated. Haden speaks of this plate as "the subtle portrait." (Page 31.) It is superb.

AMSTERDAM:
  RYKS
  MUSEUM

REMBRANDT'S MOTHER, 1628
Hind, 2.

Showing the head only, and much less convincing than No. 1. It is labored and has the worried look of something altered and changed. It was probably a Rembrandt experiment in light and dark contrast.

*REMBRANDT IN SOFT CAP. (ABOUT 1631.)
Hind, 57.

Not signed or dated but done, as Mr. Hind suggests, a little later than the etchings of his mother listed above. An excellent, clean, clear-cut etching, done with spirit and life. Never completely finished, but enough to make a brilliant etching.

SASKIA WITH PEARLS IN HAIR, 1634
Hind, 112.

This plate was perhaps started by Rembrandt, finished by pupils, and reworked later in the shop, notably in the background, back of the head and dress. It hardly represents Rembrandt, lacking as it is in force and precision of drawing. Attribution tentative.

MANASSEH BEN ISRAEL, 1636
Hind, 146.

A clear, sharp piece of etching, hard, unrelieved, and done with small feeling or sympathy. With its open masses of light it seems more like Eeckhout than Rembrandt. Moreover, the same model appears in the Death of the Virgin (Plate XI, 43—the figure between the folds of the curtain at right), an etching which I think was done by Eeckhout. It is possible that Rembrandt did the drawing and Eeckhout (a pupil in the shop in 1636) did the etching. The ill-drawn nose, the fumbled brows, the crude mouth are hardly of Rembrandt's doing. Attribution tentative.

ANSLO THE MENNONITE PREACHER, 1641
Hind, 187.

The drawing by Rembrandt for the etching is in the British Museum. The etching follows it closely but was probably done in the Rembrandt shop by pupils or assistants, principally Bol, whose manner of doing a background is here apparent. The etching has been somewhat worried, but Rembrandt was responsible for little more than its design.

*EPHRAIM BONUS, 1647
Hind, 226.

An excellent commercial etching, undoubtedly designed by Rembrandt and worked up in the shop with care and skill. It lacks freedom and spontaneity, but all the detail is there, and probably that pleased Ephraim Bonus. It is likely that Rembrandt started this etching and that more than one hand finished it.

JAN ASSELYN, PAINTER, 1647
Hind, 227.

No doubt designed and drawn by Rembrandt but executed by assistants in the shop. There are three states of it, the first showing a picture on an easel at the back. In the later states the etching is much worked over, and possibly reworked in modern times.

*Jan Six at Window, 1647
Hind, 228.

There are two drawings for this etching in the Six Collection at Amsterdam. Rembrandt undoubtedly did one, if not both, of the drawings, but how much of the etching no one is able to say. It is one of the most popular and famous of the Rembrandt etchings, and a first-state plate sold in Paris a few years ago for 70,000 francs. It is an excellent example of a shop plate, worked up to the last degree of finish in the shop, and probably thought a wonder because it outdid a steel plate in detail, and had the soft tone of a mezzotint. Those are the very things that kill its verve and spontaneity and freedom as an etching. It is a niggled plate like the little Good Samaritan and the great Christ before Pilate, and whether done with dry-point or bitten does not matter.

*Clement de Jonghe, 1651
Hind, 251.

Of these more or less formal portraits, this probably has more of Rembrandt still left in it than any of the others. It has, however, been added to in the half-dozen different states of it, and been reworked in spots. Whistler thought it a quite perfect etching.

Jan Antonides van der Linden, 1665
Hind, 268.

It should hardly be listed here with Rembrandt's etchings because it contains very little of his work. It is perfunctory shop work done for book illustration. Even the design is not original, but taken from a painting by Abraham van der Temple, now in The Hague. For an account of this etching, which was to be an engraving, see Hind's *Rembrandt's Etchings*, pp. 19 and 43.

Jacob Haaring, 1655
Hind, 287.

There is little to distinguish such work as this from that which I list hereafter as shop work, except possibly that the figure is more distinctly Rembrandt. The background of the window, with the curtain and the great mass of robes in the lower part of the plate, seem shop additions. Much worked over, and much worn down by printing.

Thomas Jacobsz Haaring, 1655
Hind, 288.

Very like the Jacob Haaring listed above. Much reworked and ruined, probably by modern hands.

*Arnold Tholinx, 1656
Hind, 289.

Rembrandt's design beyond a doubt. The likeness tallies exactly with the Rembrandt portrait of the same sitter in the Jaquemart-André Collection in Paris. The plate was perhaps worked upon in the shop by, say, Van der Pluym. The opaque shadows and the sharply contrasted high lights are much in his manner. Still it is a fine etching—almost too fine for Van der Pluym, though he was a very clever workman.

LIEVEN WILLEMSZ VAN COPPENOL, 1658
Hind, 300.

It is a carefully finished plate, done in detail as though in rivalry with copper-plate engraving, and in consequence rather lacking in spirit. Rembrandt could have had as little to do with the plate, beyond supervising it, as with the portrait in the Rothschild Collection (K.K.443) from which it is supposed to have been taken. This comes near to what I have listed hereafter as work of the Rembrandt shop, the distinction being practically without a difference.

ETCHINGS BY REMBRANDT–LIEVENS

The contention of M. André Coppier that Rembrandt and Lievens worked together on the same plates has nothing inherently improbable about it. They were together as young men, of the same age, in the same shop. Nothing could be more natural than that they should each profit by the other and perhaps each be influenced by the other. Rembrandt had no fame then, and Lievens was rather thought to be the brighter of the two. It is quite probable that they worked together, and that in the early years there was small distinction to be made between their styles. Rembrandt at the start (in his Mother's portrait (Plate III, 9)) seemed a little firmer, squarer, more angular, more direct in his line than Lievens, who was smooth, flowing, graceful, rambling. Lievens was fond of scribbling pretty curls and curves in thin, delicate traceries of the hair and beard, where Rembrandt was more summary. A difference in characterization was thus indicated, with the result that Rembrandt was forceful, comprehensive, inclusive, where Lievens was soft, weak in basic structure, and insistent upon the accidental at the expense of the more universal. It is the presence of both points of view and both methods of line-work in single plates that gives warrant for listing certain etchings as the joint product of Rembrandt and Lievens.

The matter of a joint signature suggested by M. Coppier need not be considered. Signatures on etching-plates were and are more easily fabricated than on canvases, and could be put on a plate a hundred years after the etcher's death, and as the market dictated, as readily as at the time of the original cutting of the plate. We can get on in our argument without signatures. And yet, once more, it may be said that there is nothing inherently improbable in M. Coppier's theory of a double-monogram signature.

BRITISH   *REMBRANDT'S MOTHER IN ORIENTAL HEAD-DRESS, 1631
MUSEUM   *Hind*, 51.

The costume, the head-dress with its fussy work, the small work on the hair, the fur and the back of the dress, with the peculiar drawing of the hands, all speak for Lievens. The face and general proportions of the design were probably put in by Rembrandt. Much reworked in the third state. The plate seems to be more Lievens than Rembrandt. Probably Rembrandt designed it and Lievens did most of the etching.

*REMBRANDT'S MOTHER AT TABLE, 1631
Hind, 52.

This is firmer drawing, more angular line, more positive biting than appears in No. 51. Again Lievens appears in the accessories—table, coat, head-dress, hands; and Rembrandt in the general design. Fumbled a bit in the coat and in the shadows of the head.

BEARDED MAN CALLED REMBRANDT'S FATHER, 1631
Hind, 53.

In the style of the four Oriental Heads listed hereafter, and probably with more of Lievens than Rembrandt in it. A plate by Lievens of same model, shown in reverse, is given in Rovinski, 73.

*REMBRANDT IN SOFT HAT, 1631
Hind, 54.

Many states with many additions. The Rembrandt signature was put on in the eighth state and removed in the ninth. Head by Rembrandt. Hair shows Lievens scratching and curling. The figure flattened and ill-drawn, probably by late workings or much printing.

REMBRANDT'S MOTHER IN WIDOW'S DRESS
Hind, 91.

Done with a coarse needle but in the style of Nos. 52 and 53. Much reworked. Mr. Hind thinks it the work of a pupil. Signed but not dated.

OLD MAN WITH FLOWING BEARD
Hind, 92.

A Lievens type but treated with more force and less of the pose of age than Lievens usually gives. It is probably Rembrandt and Lievens working together on the plate, with Lievens noticeable in the accessories of hand, robe, hat, and beard—especially the beard and hand. Mr. Hind observes, quite rightly, that in size and character this plate "would make a companion piece to either No. 51 or 52." Not dated.

*RAISING OF LAZARUS. (LARGER PLATE.)
Hind, 96.

This, as I have explained elsewhere (see note under Bol Etchings given to Rembrandt, Raising of Lazarus, Hind, 198), is probably the last phase of the Lazarus Resurrection. Rembrandt probably took the combined work of Lievens, Horst, and Bol, appearing in etching, drawing, and painting, and recreated this much more dignified and exalted etching, called the Larger Plate. It is highly probable that Rembrandt did no more than redesign the etching, and that the actual work on the plate was done by several hands. Eventually the plate was reworked by shop etchers, and no less than thirteen different states of it were issued. It became a mere shop machine and was printed so often

13. REMBRANDT–LIEVENS: ETCHING OF REMBRANDT'S
MOTHER AT TABLE
H. 52

14. REMBRANDT–LIEVENS: ETCHING OF REMBRANDT'S
MOTHER IN ORIENTAL COSTUME
H. 51

15. REMBRANDT–LIEVENS: ETCHING OF RAISING
OF LAZARUS
H. 96

16. REMBRANDT–LIEVENS: ETCHING OF REMBRANDT
WEARING SOFT HAT
H. 54

PLATE IV

17. REMBRANDT SHOP: ETCHING OF GOLD–WEIGHER
H. 167

18. REMBRANDT SHOP: ETCHING OF REMBRANDT AT
WINDOW
H. 229

19. REMBRANDT SHOP: ETCHING OF ST. JEROME
READING
H. 267

20. REMBRANDT SHOP: ETCHING OF ST. JEROME
BESIDE WILLOW
H. 232

PLATE V

that the plate was eventually worn smooth and became worthless. Middleton thought it invented and executed by Van Vliet; Seymour Haden thought it by Bol and Lievens. "There is no date on this plate and the signature is not Rembrandt's, nor is the *ordonnance* of the plate." (Haden, p. 34.)

AMSTERDAM:
RYKS
MUSEUM

DESCENT FROM CROSS, 1633
Hind, 103.

There has been much difference of opinion about Rembrandt's part in this plate. Middleton and Blanc doubted that it was by Rembrandt, Seymour Haden believed it by Lievens, Mr. Hind thinks it by Van Vliet, M. Coppier declares for Bol. Lievens, it is assumed, went to England about 1632, and is thought could not have done it. Why could he not have done it in 1630 or 1632, and the plate not have been signed and issued until 1633? But the date may be ignored. The plate speaks loudly for Lievens, especially in the types, the round modelling, the patterned stuffs, the hair, the effect of light. Moreover, the figure in the left foreground with the cane is the same model appearing (a head and shoulders) in an etching by Lievens in the Teyler Museum, Haarlem (No. 13). This Descent etching was probably worked up in the Rembrandt shop by several hands—perhaps Eeckhout's among others. The painting of the Descent at Munich seems to show Eeckhout in the background, but Lievens had his part in the design if not in the execution. Both etching and painting might better be called shop work because no one person was wholly responsible for either of them. Two plates exist of this subject. The first (Hind, 102) probably failed in the biting and was abandoned; the second (Hind, 103) is too much fussed over and is weak.

BRITISH
MUSEUM

OLD BEARDED MAN IN FUR CAP, 1635
Hind, 130.

It is doubted by various writers. Signed twice, and both signatures questioned. It is of a piece and by the same hand, or hands, as the Oriental Heads, that follow:

FIRST ORIENTAL HEAD, 1635
Hind, 131.

This and the following plates (Hind, 132, 133, 134) are Lievens originals (or Lievens in copy), which he probably left in the Rembrandt shop when, as supposed, he went away to England. Later, about 1634 or 1635, these plates were gotten out, worked upon in the shop, signed by Rembrandt as retouched (Rembrandt *geretuckt*), and put on the market. They are Lievens in style all through, and agree quite perfectly with the work of Lievens in etching still extant. Middleton thought them by Lievens. The hand of Rembrandt is apparent in them by faith alone. The first Head is the model called Rembrandt's Father, who died in 1630.

SECOND ORIENTAL HEAD, 1635
Hind, 132.

THIRD ORIENTAL HEAD, 1635
Hind, 133.

FOURTH ORIENTAL HEAD, 1635
Hind, 134.

REMBRANDT SHOP ETCHINGS

There are a number of etchings assigned to Rembrandt that belong to the shop, and are at best Rembrandt only in design or inspiration. No one can say who did them. Many hands at different periods have made additions and subtractions to them, until the original designer is traceable but vaguely in a point of view or a method of composition. The only thing that allies them with Rembrandt is that they probably emanated from his shop. As etchings they are mere commercial material—things worked up to please a popular taste and quite lacking in spontaneity or artistic *flair*. The best etching is sketching, not niggling over a plate in dry-point to outdo engraving. I give a dozen examples of the shop etchings.

BRITISH
MUSEUM

JAN UYTENBOGAERT, 1635
Hind, 128.

The design is probably by Backer. He was in the shop in 1635 and this is his manner of composition, as his portrait of Uytenbogaert in the Remonstrant's Meeting House in Amsterdam (reproduced in Bauch, *Backer*, Plate 24) will indicate. The etching may also be Backer's work, though the plate has been reworked in modern times to a point of disappearance so far as the original etcher is concerned. It was probably shop work—that is, composite work—from the beginning.

CHRIST BEFORE PILATE, 1635–6
Hind, 143.

Done after the *grisaille* in the National Gallery, London, which I assigned in my book on the Rembrandt paintings to Salomon Koninck. There are slight variations in this etching, but the design as it stands seems to be Koninck's. The types (particularly Pilate), the soldiers with halberds, the composition, the crowd, the monument, the architecture, the dramatic quality, the overcrowded space all point to Koninck. But who executed the plate is quite another matter. The different states indicate it was put together piece by piece, working from the sides toward the centre, and that several hands had been at work upon it with several kinds of tools besides the etching-needle. It is an elaborate and detailed surface, much fussed over until all the verve of an etching has gone from it, and the mechanical look of a copper-plate engraving alone remains. A notable illustration of a Rembrandt shop etching, in which Rembrandt himself is not apparent in any way. Middleton thought it by Bol, following the London *grisaille*, Haden thought it by Lievens, De Vries thought it by Salomon Koninck, Hind inclines to Van Vliet. It is merely shop work, with probably many hands in it at different times, and published from the Rembrandt shop for commercial gain.

*THE GOLD-WEIGHER, 1639
Hind, 167.

A good illustration of a Rembrandt shop etching—an attempt in etching to rival the detail of an engraving. Nothing about it indicates that Rembrandt had any hand in its design or execution. Seymour Haden and Middleton thought the work done by Bol, but again there is no indication of it. It has a German look about it as though designed by some German pupil of Rembrandt. The execution is shop work, with several hands, early and late, noticeable in it. It has been worked from the sides toward the centre by pupils, with the possible thought of a master putting in the principal head. "N'est pas tout entière de la main de Rembrandt" (Blanc, p. 198).

MAN WITH CROSS AND CHAIN, 1641
Hind, 189.

Much worried in the background. Same model as the Card Player (Hind, 190). Design and execution by pupils.

THE OMVAL, 1645
Hind, 210.

The drawing for this etching is in the Louvre. Both drawing and etching in design probably by Rembrandt, and excellent in every way. The etching probably worked upon in the shop. The figures at left may be a later addition.

JAN CORNELIS SYLVIUS, PREACHER, 1646
Hind, 225.

A Rembrandt sketch for this etching in the British Museum (Hind, B. M., 65). The shadow of the head and hand on the frame was, no doubt, added in the shop—an artistic incongruity that perhaps Rembrandt passed with a smile, if he ever saw it. Detailed shop work. Said to have been done from a picture painted in 1644. Sylvius died in 1639.

*REMBRANDT AT WINDOW, 1648
Hind, 229.

Much altered and amended through half a dozen states. The whole plate blackish, hard, and rather woodeny as a result of much working. Originally, no doubt, an excellent design, which Rembrandt may have supervised.

*ST. JEROME BESIDE POLLARD WILLOW, 1648
Hind, 232.

This etching seems harder than the drawing (Hind, D., XXII) which may have been used in connection with it. It is sketchy, blackish, deeply bitten, and is evidently of shop origin. It should be compared with the Omval etching (Hind, 210) not only for the likenesses but for the differences.

FAUST IN HIS STUDY, 1652
Hind, 260.

The design suggests Van der Pluym—the chief factotum in the Rembrandt shop after 1650. The execution also is in the Van der Pluym manner, with large flat spaces of pure light in contrast with patches of dense black. But the plate probably came out of the Rembrandt shop after several hands had worked upon it—especially in its background.   One of the hands may have been that of Aert de Gelder.

*St. Jerome Reading, 1653
Hind, 267.

The Rembrandt drawing for this etching is in the Kunsthalle, Hamburg, and is no doubt genuine.   The etching itself is of excellent quality, almost too good to be listed as shop work.   Rembrandt probably did some of the work on the plate, but much of the landscape, especially in the shadowed portions, has a worried look as though several hands had gone over it.   Still it remains one of the notable etchings in the *œuvre*.

Lieven Willemsz van Coppenol, 1653
Hind, 269.

The smaller plate of Coppenol, of which there are half a dozen states —the later states, beginning with the third, much reworked.   It seems a mere shop pot-boiler.

Four Illustrations to a Spanish Book, 1655
Hind, 284.

Shop designs and shop work throughout.

Jan Lutma, 1656
Hind, 290.

The design probably Rembrandt's.   The added window in the second state, which wrecks the original scheme of light as shown in the first state, is a shop addition.

Abraham Francken, 1656?
Hind, 291.

There are many states of this etching, and all of them, even from the first, rather muddled in their workmanship.   There has been much alteration and many hands at work.   The plate clears up in the last states, but is still an overworked, tortured production, with the head always out of value.

St. Francis Praying Beneath Tree, 1657
Hind, 292.

There are two states of this etching, the first unfinished, and the second finished in part in a bungling, perfunctory manner, probably by a later hand.   Two signatures of Rembrandt.   Compare this etching with those listed above, Hind, 267, 210, 232.

The Phœnix, 1658
Hind, 295.

Shop work throughout, the same as Hind, 284.

CHAPTER VI

THE PUPILS AND FOLLOWERS

I HAVE suggested several times that the works of the pupils and followers, in both drawing and etching, are more easily detached from the mass of the *œuvre* and assembled by themselves than those of the master. The pupils have less skill, are less resourceful, more mannered in their themes, their compositions, their types. Moreover, each one of them, in his sketches, has some peculiarity of drawing or arrangement, some spreading of ink with pen or thumb, some pattern of light and dark that he keeps repeating. Bol, one of the best of the pupils, for example, is mannered with his kneeling figures, their upraised hands, the drawing of the thumb, and the points of the fingers; Eeckhout repeats himself in types, often using the same models in his paintings, drawings, and etchings, and is mannered in his poses, gestures, loops of costume, arabesques of lines; Lievens has a fancy for old men with flowing beards and dishevelled hair, in which he ploughs with the sharp wooden end of the brush, or scratches with the pen or the needle. These small features are often the catch-points from which one gets a first start, as I shall endeavor to show in the notes that follow. When, with these catch-points as first clews, the paintings, drawings, and etchings of one supposed individuality are collected and brought together they often make for agreement in a very positive way.

In the lists that follow, both for drawings and etchings, and alike for master and pupil, I have grouped the works of a kind and a quality that indicate a common origin with some one individual. Wherever I have been able to associate several drawings or etchings evidently by the same hand, and cannot name the artist, I have kept them in a group and given the group a letter. This notation was followed in my book on the Rembrandt paintings, and I am now, so far as possible, relating and connecting the numbers there with the letters here. If the time shall ever arrive when these groups can receive a name instead of a number or a letter, the substitution can be made, but it is not worth while to force probability by assuming names from among Rembrandt's pupils or contemporaries. For example, the landscapes assigned to Rembrandt might be dealt out arbitrarily, or upon some slight resemblances, to Molyn, to Seghers, to Philip Koninck, or even to J. G. Cuyp, but that would be merely establishing new card houses for future demolition. Whenever I have attached a new name it has usually been done with some probability or plausibility, but even then I have often added a question-mark, indicating that there may be doubt. The groups, each one disclosing a distinct individuality, are the primary consideration. Whether each group receives a name or a number or a letter is of secondary importance.

Some seventeenth-century drawings (not belonging to the Rembrandt school) have been given to the Rembrandt pupils by various connoisseurs perhaps for lack of a better goal. Usually they have been assigned without much consideration. Not a few of them have been given to pupils following erroneous precedents. For example, some collector, having a number of landscape drawings which he thought were by Eeckhout, had them signed with Eeckhout's name. That, having established a false Eeckhout criterion, has led to other landscapes of the same kind being put down to Eeckhout, until now there are a score of these drawings given to him that do not belong to him. The drawings are crude juvenile performances that almost any third-rate painter might have done, whereas Eeckhout was a learned painter and shows in his paintings a rather profound knowledge of landscape—something, at any rate, quite different from these stick-like pen drawings for which he is now held responsible.

Again, there has been some assignment of drawings to pupils such as Bol, Lievens, and Flinck, because their names were very well known, and they themselves were among the near-great. But there has been little or nothing given to such unknowns as Drost, Horst, Wulfhagen, Rodermondt, Renesse, and a dozen others who worked in the Rembrandt shop, and presumably did drawings and etchings not inferior in numbers to those of Bol or Flinck. As a result, the Bols and Flincks are greatly confused by many contradictory assignments, and the Drosts and Horsts are left hanging in the air with nothing whatever to their account.

I have had to ignore most of these assignments to pupils and to establish my own attributions by carefully comparing the etchings and drawings with the paintings. It is usual to work from the drawings up to the paintings, but it is quite possible to reverse that order and arrive at similar results. But not in every case, by any means. There are numbers of etchings, in and out of the Rembrandt *œuvre*, that might be given tentatively to two or three different hands with some show of reason. But such assignments cannot be accepted as final. Unless a probability can be established, perhaps it is better to pass over questionable etchings for the time being. And for my purpose a dozen drawings or etchings by one hand in a group is measurably satisfactory and sufficient. It is not absolutely necessary to run down, capture, and pigeonhole every scratch of the pen or needle by that hand. The quality of a wine can be gathered from a glass of it as well as from a whole bottle. But, of course, there are those who think the whole bottle should be emptied before one is competent to judge of it. My book on the Rembrandt paintings was quite as much abused for what was ignored as for what was recorded.

But the reader need not infer that because I do not catalogue or comment on certain drawings that I have not considered them. The etchings and drawings in the Rembrandt *œuvre*, and those by his pupils, are well known, have been published in various forms of reproductions, and almost all of the originals are in public museums where they are accessible. Every one interested in art knows them in one form or another. It is from them that the history of Rembrandt and his school will ultimately be made up, and not from the odd drawings here and there that happen to be in private possession. But even these private holdings are now known in reproductions, from which the student may get an accurate knowledge if he is not able to consult the originals.

CHAPTER VII

DRAWINGS AND ETCHINGS BY REMBRANDT PUPILS

JACOB ADRIAENSZ BACKER
1608–1651

BACKER, who was early in the Rembrandt shop, must have produced etchings and drawings, in and out of the Rembrandt shop, but there are few of them recognizable to-day. There is a drawing given to him in the Albertina, Vienna, a Portrait of a Lady (Meder, 950), but it is not entirely in the Rembrandt vein. Also in the British Museum (Sheepshank Collection) there are five etchings of nude nymphs put down to him, but all of them are in the classical Antwerp manner, and none of them are representative of Backer, the pupil of Rembrandt. There are paintings in this manner also given to Backer, but there must be some mistake about them. They are probably by another of the name. The portraits by the Rembrandt Backer are as unmistakably in the Rembrandt manner as the Antwerp portraits and nymphs are not. In the Dresden Gallery is a drawing of an Old Man with Hand on Breast (Lilienfeld, Dresden, 51) which might be given to Backer. It is the drawing for the Swalmius portrait at Antwerp (K.K.214), which I had the temerity of soul to assign to Backer in my first Rembrandt book. There is also at the Ryks Museum, Amsterdam, the drawing for the large picture of the Governors of the Nieuwezijds Huiszittenhuis. The Rembrandt etching of Uytenbogaert (Hind, 128) was probably taken from a Backer design. But more than these I can find nothing of his that can be identified with any certainty.

LEENDERT CORNELIS VAN BEYEREN
1620–1649

Van Beyeren was a pupil in the Rembrandt shop between 1635 and 1638 who is supposed to have copied Rembrandt's pictures and done other shop work. On the reverse of a red-chalk drawing in the Berlin Print Room (given to Rembrandt but by Lastman) of Susanna and the Elders (Plate XLVIII, 189) there is an inscription, said to be in Rembrandt's handwriting, giving the titles of certain pupil drawings which were sold, supposedly by Rembrandt. The amount for each drawing is given. One

44

item is a Flora by Leendert, put down at five florins.[1]   This pupil also figures at auction sales in Rembrandt's interest,[2] his name is on inventories of Rembrandt copies,[3] and he appears elsewhere in Rembrandt documents;[4] and yet nothing of his—drawing, etching, painting—is publicly known at the present day.   What became of his work?   If the inscription above is authentic, it would suggest that his pictures were sold as shop product.   As for his drawings, they were probably put into the Rembrandt portfolios and later on inventoried, and finally sold as Rembrandts.   His etched work we can only guess at.   Was it put upon the Rembrandt plates, and finally worked over and worked out by later hands?   Who knows?

FERDINAND BOL
1616–1680

With Bol we come to a Rembrandt pupil whose work can be positively identified.   A number of his pictures, plates, and drawings still survive under his own name.   They are probably not his best work—that having long ago been transferred to Rembrandt.   Mr. Fry argues[5] that of half a dozen pictures by Bol, conceived, composed, and executed in one vein— the composition being merely varied—the best of the half-dozen is by Rembrandt, and the rest is merely Bol following Rembrandt.   The Tobias and the Angel in the Louvre is thus a Rembrandt, but the Copenhagen and Liverpool variations of the same composition and types are by Bol. The Horst Danae at Petrograd (Leningrad) is by Rembrandt, but again the half-dozen repetitions of the composition at Berlin, Dublin, and Dulwich are by Horst, who is following and imitating the Danae.   The Maes Old Woman Cutting Her Nails is by Rembrandt, but the half-dozen repetitions of that type, color, drawing, and handling are by Maes following Rembrandt.   With this argument carried to its logical conclusion, Rembrandt set a separate pace and pattern for each one of his seventy or more pupils that was different from any and all of the others.   This pace and pattern seemed, for some unaccountable reason, to agree with and reflect exactly the individuality of each pupil, and was never set for, or imitated, or followed by any other pupil.   Rembrandt thus revealed himself as a man of seventy different individualities, seventy points of view, and seventy different methods of working—an utterly impossible person.

Rembrandt worked in only one style (with variations), as did Titian, Velasquez, Frans Hals, Holbein.   The pictures, drawings, and etchings

---

[1] Hofstede de Groot, *Die Urkunden über Rembrandt*, p. 39.   [2] *Ibid.*, p. 52.   [3] *Ibid.*, p. 58.
[4] *Ibid.*, pp. 155, 386.   [5] The *Burlington Magazine*, April, 1924.

which I have assigned to him indicate this. He could not work in any other way. If the Tobias and the Angel in the Louvre, the Danae of the Hermitage, and the Old Woman Cutting Her Nails in the Metropolitan were brought together they would reveal three absolutely different and distinct styles that contradict and defy each other. It is not possible that any one hand painted all three. And it was never necessary to assume it except in the interests of collector and dealer. The pictures, as named, agree perfectly with the respective styles of Bol, Horst, and Maes; they fit in with their works, and are the strong pictures of their output. They do not agree at all with the Rembrandt pictures except in a general school likeness, which was shown in the works of all the pupils.

At any rate as regards Bol, what was not strong enough to sell as a Rembrandt has been graciously left to Bol's account—there being no other use for it. It is not forceful enough to account for Bol's reputation in his own time, but it is something from which we can work to a better understanding of the man. None of it is dated before 1642, when Bol was twenty-six. He was in the Rembrandt shop before 1635, for at that date Rembrandt was selling his (Bol's) pictures from the shop,[1] and he probably remained there as a shop assistant until about 1642. All his work during those years is under the Rembrandt name or has disappeared from view. I have already referred to the Hague Guild rule prohibiting apprentices in the shop from signing their own name to their own works while working in the shop. That probably accounts for the Bol work not being signed until 1642, when he left Rembrandt and started for himself.

He was a facile and ingenious workman, and as the first assistant he, no doubt, prepared and superintended much of the work turned out of the Rembrandt shop during his time. Haden thought him the nearest of all to Rembrandt. "It is extremely difficult to say of two things at once so similar and dissimilar—this is by Rembrandt and this by Bol" (Haden, p. 23). Some of his etchings and drawings now under Rembrandt's name, I shall endeavor to identify herein. The large number assigned him is accounted for by his long years in the Rembrandt shop as assistant.

DRAWINGS BY BOL

AMSTERDAM:
RYKS
MUSEUM

JOSEPH PRESENTING JACOB TO PHARAOH
A276.

It is a pen drawing, with wash and color, a little scratchy and with pot-hooks, but quite in Bol's manner. It agrees with the Bol picture at Dresden, Jacob Before Pharaoh.

[1] Hofstede de Groot, *Die Urkunden über Rembrandt*, p. 39.

Oriental Figure Seated, with Turban
A2546.

The drawing is little more than suggestive of Bol, and is tentatively listed here.

Ascension of Christ
A3352.

A large, well-done, washed drawing, with upraised hands and kneeling figures in the Bol manner. It is probably his work.

BREMEN:
KUNSTHALLE

Admiral De Ruyter
Pauli, vol. 2, No. 13.

The sketch for the Ryks Museum portrait.

HAARLEM:
TEYLER
MUSEUM

*Abraham Kneeling
Kleinmann, Series IV, 36.

Almost certainly by Bol.

LONDON:
BRITISH
MUSEUM

Holy Family
Hind, B. M., 1, p. 61, Pl. XXIX.

A study for the etching (Bartsch, 4), but both etching and drawing more in the manner of Van der Pluym than Bol.

Jacob's Dream
Hind, B. M., 2, p. 61, Pl. XXX.

A poor, weak drawing, almost too poor for Bol. Done in pen and sepia. Attribution questionable.

Jacob's Dream
Hind, B. M., 3, p. 61, Pl. XXX.

It is probably Bol's work, but not his best work. Done in pen and sepia. Attribution questionable.

Portrait of Lady
Hind, B. M., 4, p. 62, Pl. XXIX.

A very good drawing, done in sepia with a brush, and slightly different, of course, from the Bol pen drawings.

DRAWINGS BY BOL GIVEN TO REMBRANDT

AMSTERDAM:
RYKS
MUSEUM

Pyramus and Thisbe
Lilienfeld, Amsterdam, 21.

It is almost certainly Bol in the kneeling figure, the upraised hands with the mannered finger-points, the scrubbed background. The almost formless reclining figure is again like Bol's work.

AMSTERDAM:
JAN SIX
COLLECTION

Joseph Relating the Dream
Valentiner, vol. I, 87.

Note the emphasized dog or other object in right lower corner. Bol often repeats this round object in this place, with swift, strong pen lines.

AMSTERDAM:
FODOR
MUSEUM

ESAU SELLING HIS BIRTHRIGHT
Hind, D., XVII; Valentiner, vol. I, 55.

To be closely compared with the Old Man Seated in Chair in the British Museum (Hind, B. M., p. 28; Michel, vol. 2, p. 213). They are by the same hand.

ASCHAFFEN-
BURG
LIBRARY

ANGEL APPEARING TO MANOAH
Valentiner, vol. I, XVII.

Given to Bol by Doctor Valentiner.

BERLIN:
KAISER-
FRIEDRICH
MUSEUM

JACOB AND JOSEPH'S BLOODY COAT
Valentiner, vol. I, 97.

Done with much spirit and in manner not unlike Flinck or Eeckhout. The dark figure at left should be noted. It is a Bol mannerism appearing frequently in his work.

ANGEL LEAVING MANOAH AND WIFE
Lilienfeld, Berlin, 15.

The angel much in Bol's style. The types are the same as in the Old Man Seated in Chair (Valentiner, vol. I, 89). A swift sketch given with verve.

ABRAHAM'S SACRIFICE
Lilienfeld, Berlin, 7; Valentiner, vol. I, 49.

With Bol's scribbling in the background landscape. In agreement with the Bol Abraham at Haarlem. Note the similar pose of the Abraham.

SARAH AND HAGAR
Lilienfeld, Berlin, 3.

It has the same back drawing, the same hooked and angled lines, as the drawing in the British Museum of Rembrandt drawing from a Model (H., B. M., p. 31), which, with the etching, I think by Bol. (See the note following under British Museum drawings.) This drawing is weak and may be by some Bol follower. Assignment tentative.

TOBIAS AND THE FISH
Lilienfeld, Berlin, 26; Valentiner, vol. I, 235.

With Bol's drawing, scribbling, round finger-tips and angle-hooks. There is little doubt of its being by Bol. In agreement with the Abraham at Berlin (Lilienfeld, 7).

A BEWAILING IN MOUNTAIN LANDSCAPE
Lilienfeld, Berlin, 87.

This drawing again shows the mannerisms of Bol. Note the hands upraised, and the reinforced figure in right foreground.

JACOB'S DREAM
Lilienfeld, Berlin, 10a.

An early study perhaps for the Bol painting of Jacob's Dream at Dresden, somewhat varied and reversed in the figures, but with practically the same types, attitudes, and properties. Another stronger study of the same subject in the Louvre (Valentiner, vol. I, 72).

BERLIN:
KAPPEL
COLLECTION

ANGEL WITH MANOAH AND WIFE
Valentiner, vol. I, 132.

BREMEN:
KUNSTHALLE

THE ANNUNCIATION
739; Lippmann, Third Series, 132.

The Madonna with upraised hands and mannered fingers. These drawings at Berlin and Bremen all have the same spirit and the same mannerisms of drawing. If put together in reproductions they will affirm and confirm each other. A "Good Samaritan" drawing in this Bremen gallery might be given to Bol with a query.

BRUNSWICK
MUSEUM

ST. JEROME
It is possibly by Bol.

CHATSWORTH:
DEVONSHIRE
COLLECTION

DAVID AND SOLOMON
Valentiner, vol. I, 174.
Assignment tentative.

DRESDEN
MUSEUM

RAPE OF GANYMEDE
Lilienfeld, Dresden, 47.

This drawing is a study for the Bol (given to Rembrandt) picture of Ganymede in the Dresden Museum. It has the usual wriggling, pothooked lines as in other Bol drawings. Another version in the Dresden Museum, probably some student's study of the picture (Michel, vol. I, p. 222). Both picture and drawing by Bol.

APOSTLE APPEALING
Hind, D., 1.

It is possibly a study for the etching given to Rembrandt (Hind, 5). The etching is, I think, by Bol, and perhaps this drawing belongs also to Bol, but it is not in his usual manner. It is a black-chalk drawing, which gives a different line and surface from pen-and-ink, and these may mislead; but an undoubted Bol in black chalk, Abraham's Sacrifice, listed below under British Museum drawings, should be used for comparison. It shows more wriggling of line and scribbling than this Apostle Appealing, which seems too direct and simple for Bol. Attribution tentative.

MADONNA AND CHILD
Valentiner, vol. I, 322; Lilienfeld, Dresden, 16.

To be closely compared with three drawings in the Hofstede de Groot Collection at The Hague, reproduced in Valentiner, vol. I, 149, 158, 302. They are of unequal quality.

HAARLEM:
KOENIGS
COLLECTION

ABRAHAM AND THE ANGELS
Valentiner, vol. I, XV.

Study for the Petrograd picture given to Rembrandt, but by Bol (K.K.181). Note the type looking in door at back. It appears elsewhere in Bol's drawings, notably in the one reproduced in Michel, vol. I, p. 213.   Given to Bol by Doctor Valentiner.

HAARLEM:
TEYLER
MUSEUM

RETURN OF PRODIGAL
Valentiner, vol. I, 388; Hind, D., VIII.

This is the Bol model and also the Bol manner, especially in the swift, strong lines in the figure of the Prodigal and in the kneeling attitude.   The background is rubbed in with wash.   Many of Bol's drawings seem to have affinity with those of Flinck and Eeckhout.   All three of them were in the Rembrandt shop about the same time (1635 and after), which may account for some likenesses.   There are Flinck likenesses in this drawing of the Prodigal.   Mr. Hind thinks this a study for the etching of the same subject (Hind, 147).

THE HAGUE:
H. DE GROOT
COLLECTION

*GOD APPEARS TO ABRAHAM
Valentiner, vol. I, 8.

This is possibly the first of three studies made by Bol of the same theme—the other two being in the Victoria and Albert Museum (Valentiner, vol. I, XVIII) and the Albertina, Vienna (Valentiner, vol. I, 7). Note the emphasized kneeling figure at right.   Bol keeps repeating this composition with a low object at right, put in with swift, rounded lines.

FINDING OF MOSES
Valentiner, vol. I, 123.

A slight but spirited drawing by Bol, much better than three-quarters of the drawings assigned to Rembrandt.

JONATHAN AND DAVID
Valentiner, vol. I, 158.

I have seen only the reproductions of this and the other listed drawings in the De Groot Collection.   This one agrees in part with the Madonna and Child (Valentiner, vol. I, 302 and 322).

BOAZ AND RUTH
Valentiner, vol. I, 149.

STUDY FOR ADORATION OF KINGS
Valentiner, vol. I, 302.

Thought by Doctor de Groot a study for the Buckingham Palace picture (K.K.387), but the resemblance seems superficial.

HAMBURG:
KUNSTHALLE

HAGAR AND ISHMAEL
Valentiner, vol. I, 31.

Probably a second study of this subject by Bol—the first being at Munich (Valentiner, vol. I, 30).

*JOSEPH IN PRISON INTERPRETING THE DREAM
Valentiner, vol. I, XIV.

A second and final study for Bol's picture of the same subject at the Schwerin Museum.   Formerly to Bol, but given to Rembrandt by Doctor de Groot (H. de G., 343) and Bol using the drawing for his picture at Schwerin. The same old story. Doctor Valentiner restored the drawing to Bol in his first volume of Rembrandt's drawings.

ABRAHAM'S SACRIFICE
Hind, B. M., 6; Bell, I; Valentiner, vol. I, 48.

This is Bol as he draws with black chalk. The vise-like right hand is such a pronounced Bol mannerism that it alone would seem to carry conviction. The drawing is a sketch for the picture the Sacrifice of Isaac at Munich, which is given to Rembrandt, but which I assigned to Bol. There is much unanimity of opinion among critics that this picture was done by Bol when in Rembrandt's shop (1636), and that the inscription saying that Rembrandt retouched it is negligible.

EXPULSION OF HAGAR AND ISHMAEL
Hind, B. M., 23; Bell, XXIII; Valentiner, vol. I, 20.

In Bol's manner and with his models, though Eeckhout, in the Rembrandt shop at the same time (1634–1640), confuses the record by adopting at times Bol's method and manner. Evidently they both used the same shop model that appears here as Abraham. Notice the Bol lines terminating in hooks, also the finger-tips of the Abraham.

*ARTIST DRAWING FROM MODEL
Hind, D., XXVIII.

With lines ending in hooks and a washed background. Quite in Bol's style and agreeing with the drawing on the reverse of the sheet, which is a sketch for Bol's Schwerin Museum picture of Joseph Interpreting the Dream. This sketch on the reverse (Valentiner, vol. I, 108) does not necessarily prove the obverse to be by Bol also, but taken in connection with the close analogies in the style of both drawings it may be accepted as contributory evidence. The obverse is a drawing for the etching (Hind, 231) given to Rembrandt, but by Bol. Note the emphasized figure at right with strong lines and bunched form—the same effect being produced in Bol's other drawings by a kneeling figure, a dog or a cat.

JOSEPH IN PRISON INTERPRETING THE DREAM
Valentiner, vol. I, 108.

With Bol's types, especially the Joseph, and with round finger-tips and emphasized lines in figures at the right. Perhaps a first attempt at this subject, and changed in the second drawing of the same subject at Hamburg (Valentiner, vol. I, XIV). This is the reverse of the drawing just listed (Hind, D., XXVIII)—the sketch for the Schwerin Museum picture by Bol.

ABRAHAM AND ANGEL
Hind, B. M., addition after 39.

In pen, sepia, wash, and water-color.

CHRIST WALKING ON THE WATER
Hind, B. M., p. 32; Valentiner, vol. I, 425.

There is a second drawing of the same subject in the British Museum (Hind, B. M., 73) which seems to be a shop sketch following this one. It is coarser and less sure. Compare with God Appearing to Abraham in Victoria and Albert Museum (Valentiner, vol. I, XVIII).

OLD MAN SEATED IN ARMCHAIR
Hind, B. M., p. 28; Michel, vol. 2, p. 213; Valentiner, vol. I, 89.

Mr. Hind notes that Bol uses this model of the Old Man in his etchings (B., 7 and 10). But this drawing is by Bol, too. Note the likeness in types between the two men in this drawing and those in the Berlin drawing Angel Leaving Manoah (Lilienfeld, Berlin, 15) and the Haarlem drawing of Abraham and Angels (Valentiner, vol. I, XV)— the head looking in at the back. Note in this drawing the emphasized and rounded cat at right.

LONDON:
VICTORIA
AND ALBERT
MUSEUM

*GOD APPEARING TO ABRAHAM
Valentiner, vol. I, XVIII.

Compare with same subject by Bol reproduced in Valentiner, vol. I, 7 and 8. Note the crouching figure of Abraham. That crouching figure of man, dog, or cat appears frequently in these Bol drawings. And done always with the same sharp black lines. Given to Bol by Doctor Valentiner.

LONDON:
NORTHWICK
COLLECTION

HAMAN AND AHASUERUS
Valentiner, vol. I, 205.

Note the type, the round finger-tips, the pot-hooks of Bol.

LONDON:
LADY LUCAS
COLLECTION

PASTORAL

With the Bol mannered finger-tips.

MUNICH:
OLD
PINACOTHEK

HAGAR AND ISHMAEL IN WILDERNESS
Valentiner, vol. I, 30.

JACOB AND JOSEPH'S BLOODY COAT
Valentiner, vol. I, 95.

In agreement with a drawing of the same theme at Berlin (Valentiner, vol. I, 97).

PARIS:
LOUVRE

TOBIAS AND ANGEL
No. 22978.

With old and new ink on the same sheet.

JACOB'S DREAM
No. 22881; Valentiner, vol. I, 72.

With upraised hands and mannered finger-tips as in other drawings by Bol. This is probably the first thought for the Bol drawing for the signed Bol picture of Jacob's Dream in the Old Pinacothek, Munich. Of course it will be said that the drawing is by Rembrandt, and that Bol did the picture after his master's drawing, but there is nothing about either drawing or picture that Bol could not do. Both are wholly in his manner and not at all in Rembrandt's manner.

21. BOL: PAINTING OF JOSEPH INTERPRETING THE DREAM
Schwerin Museum

22. BOL (GIVEN TO REMBRANDT): DRAWING OF JOSEPH
INTERPRETING THE DREAM
Kunsthalle, Hamburg

23. BOL (GIVEN TO REMBRANDT): DRAWING OF GOD
APPEARING TO ABRAHAM
Victoria and Albert Museum, London

24. BOL (GIVEN TO REMBRANDT): DRAWING OF GOD
APPEARING TO ABRAHAM
H. de Groot Collection, The Hague

PLATE VI

25. BOL (GIVEN TO REMBRANDT): DRAWING OF ARTIST
DRAWING FROM MODEL
British Museum, London

26. BOL (GIVEN TO REMBRANDT): ETCHING OF ARTIST
DRAWING FROM MODEL
H. 231

27. BOL (GIVEN TO REMBRANDT): DRAWING OF JEWISH
BRIDE
Stockholm Museum

28. BOL (GIVEN TO REMBRANDT): ETCHING OF JEWISH
BRIDE
H. 127

PLATE VII

29. BOL: PAINTING OF PORTRAIT OF FLINCK
Old Pinacothek, Munich

30. BOL (GIVEN TO REMBRANDT): ETCHING OF
REMBRANDT LEANING ON STONE SILL
H. 168

31. BOL: DRAWING OF ABRAHAM KNEELING
Teyler Museum, Haarlem

32. BOL (GIVEN TO REMBRANDT): DRAWING OF TOBIAS AND
FAMILY WITH ANGEL
Albertina, Vienna

PLATE VIII

The Unfaithful Servant
Valentiner, vol. I, 366a.

The kneeling figure is the clew to be followed, as in several other drawings by Bol listed herein.

PARIS:
LOUVRE,
BONNAT
COLLECTION

Beheading of John the Baptist
Valentiner, vol. I, 278.

A slight but very spirited drawing.

PARIS:
BIBLIOTHÈQUE
NATIONALE

Jacob's Blessing

Attribution tentative.

PARIS:
JOSEPH
REINACH
COLLECTION

Tobit Recovering Sight
Valentiner, vol. I, 252.

The drawing of the back of the woman at the right and the long lines suggest Bol. Assignment tentative.

STOCKHOLM
MUSEUM

*Jewish Bride
Lippmann, Second Series, 18; Kruse, IV, 15; Michel, vol. I, 221.

A study for the etching (Hind, 127), a palpable Bol, given to Rembrandt, as is also this drawing, but both drawing and etching are by Bol.

Tobias and Angel
Kruse, I, 16.

Angel, with Manoah and Wife
Valentiner, vol. I, 135.

Attribution tentative.

Abraham and Isaac
Kruse, I, 4; Valentiner, vol. I, 46.

VIENNA:
ALBERTINA

*Tobias and Family with Angel
Meder, 152; Michel, vol. 2, p. 62.

A Bol washed drawing with kneeling figures, upraised hands, and mannered finger-tips. The same types as in the Tobias and Angel picture of the Louvre, the Bol Three Maries at Copenhagen, and the Liverpool Bol. It goes along with and is confirmed by those pictures. Listed in the Albertina as belonging to Rembrandt's school. See the etching in Hind, 185, given to Rembrandt, but by Bol, which follows this drawing in reverse with slight variations. Doctor de Groot lists the drawing under Rembrandt (1410), but adds: "Nicht ganz sicher."

Group of Orientals
Meder, 1320.

Probably by the same hand (Bol's) that did the drawing of Rembrandt Drawing a Model. The drawing of the baggy garments is the same in both drawings. Assignment tentative.

REBECCA AT WELL
Valentiner, vol. I, 51.

Assignment tentative.

TOBIAS AND ANGEL
Valentiner, vol. I, 239.

Assignment tentative.

GOD APPEARING TO ABRAHAM
Valentiner, vol. I, 7.

Probably the last of several drawings by Bol of this theme. The drawing has been prettified by a later hand. It is retouched in the foreground and the sky has been toned. The strength of the earlier drawing (Valentiner, vol. I, 8) is lost.

THE TOILET
Meder, 215.

The same model and method as in the Jewish Bride (Kruse, IV, 15).

JACOB'S DREAM
Meder, 125.

A red-chalk study for Bol's Dresden picture of the same title. Another drawing of the theme in Berlin Museum (Lilienfeld, Berlin, 10a).

ETCHINGS BY BOL

AMSTERDAM:
RYKS MUSEUM

ABRAHAM'S SACRIFICE
Bartsch, 1.

Large, signed, no date, scratchy and cobwebby at back, but well done. Bol beyond doubt.

GIDEON'S SACRIFICE
Bartsch, 2.

With Bol's angel and wood interior for background. See the note under Bol's Etchings (given to Rembrandt), the Angel Leaving Tobias and Family (Hind, 185).

MADONNA, CHILD, AND JOSEPH
Bartsch, 4.

This seems more like Van der Pluym than Bol. It is not signed, and the assignment to Bol here is tentative.

OLD MAN WITH GLASSES IN HAND
Bartsch, 5.

With cobweb background, finely lined hair, and the texture of garments insisted upon.

SCHOLAR AT TABLE
Bartsch, 6.

It looks somewhat like a Lievens, though signed and dated 1642, with wiry small hair upon head and beard. Three states.

ASTROLOGER
Bartsch, 8.

Assignment tentative. It has the look of a Koninck.

OLD MAN WITH VELVET HAT
Bartsch, 9.

Signed 1642.

OLD MAN WITH HAT
Bartsch, 10.

Again the cobweb background, curled hair, and small lines of the etching-needle.

OFFICER WITH STEEL COLLAR AND PLUME
Bartsch, 11.

An etching that might easily pass as a Rembrandt with the un-initiated. Note again the cobweb ground and scratchy hair.

YOUNG MAN IN HAT
Bartsch, 12.

MAN WITH VELVET HAT
Bartsch, 13.

Signed 1642 and Rembrandtesque in manner.

WOMAN AT WINDOW
Bartsch, 14.

With velvety textures peculiar to Bol.

WOMAN IN HAT
Bartsch, 15.

A profile very well done. Signed 1644; two states.

PHILOSOPHER AT TABLE
Bartsch, 16.

It is suggestive of Koninck, though a signed Bol. Worried some-what in handling.

OLD MAN WITH BEARD
Bartsch, 17.

It is suggestive of Lievens.

BRITISH
MUSEUM

ST. JEROME
Rovinski, 3.

OLD MAN SEATED
Rovinski, 7.

HOUR OF DEATH
Rovinski, 18.

Not a good Bol, but undoubtedly genuine.

OLD MAN WARMING HANDS
Rovinski, 19.

Signature false. In manner of Lievens.

ETCHINGS BY BOL GIVEN TO REMBRANDT
OR OTHERS

PETER AND JOHN AT THE GATE
Hind, 5.

A coarse scribbled plate with a characteristic Bol hand and fingers, and an ineffective background. Assignment tentative. Coppier lists it among pieces erroneously attributed to Rembrandt. Also attributed to Lievens.

FLIGHT INTO EGYPT
Hind, 17.

The first state of the plate shows work similar to the Peter and John (Hind, 5) listed above. There are six states and a number of changes, the plate being cut down after the first state. Blanc thought the Joseph reworked by Van Vliet.

HOLY FAMILY
Hind, 95.

Compare with Bol's picture the Flight into Egypt in the Dresden Gallery. The figures are reversed and slightly varied in the etching, but the models are the same. Note the similar drawing of the Madonna's right hand, the face and head-dress. Also note that the basket with the cloth is repeated. Joseph's hat is the same as in the etching (Hind, 17) given above.

FLIGHT INTO EGYPT. (SMALL PLATE.)
Hind, 105.

Much worked over, probably by later hands. Haden thought it by Bol. He possibly had a hand in it, but the assignment here is tentative.

*THE GREAT JEWISH BRIDE
Hind, 127.

The vise-like grip of the right hand is a pronounced and convincing Bol mannerism. The curled and twisted hair, the velvety robe, the hatched background all speak rather positively for Bol. Four states. A so-called study or first state for this etching is among the Rejected Rembrandt Etchings (Hind, 361). Rovinski made out a Bol signature on the chest.

RETURN OF THE PRODIGAL
Hind, 147.

With certain Bol features in the foreground and background, and yet the etching is not positively by Bol. There are likenesses here to Flinck and Eeckhout. See the Bol drawing in Hind, D., VIII, which may have been a study for this etching. Attribution tentative.

STUDY OF SASKIA AS ST. CATHERINE
Hind, 154.

The so-called "Little Jewish Bride." The type, the shading of the face, the curling hair, the hand—particularly the hand—suggest analogies with the Great Jewish Bride (Hind, 127) listed above. It is the same kind of work but not carried so far as the Hind, 127.

REMBRANDT WITH VELVET CAP
Hind, 156.

Rembrandt must have been a man with a very changeable face to meet all the different likenesses of him in painting and etching. Here he looks like a German swashbuckler, and has a bravo air, than which nothing was more foreign to Rembrandt the artist. Rovinski reproduces the same type and model, and assigns it to Bol. The so-called Rembrandt etching (Hind, 156) is very Bol-like in its pose, type, and work, but it is also a little in the manner of Salomon Koninck. Attribution tentative.

*REMBRANDT LEANING ON STONE SILL
Hind, 168.

This etching has things in common with the Bol etching of an Officer (Bartsch, 11). The model and the pose is the same in both etchings. Here also is the Bol flowing hair, curled and twisted with many lines of the needle, the Bol velvety textures and mannered folds of the robe, the cobweb hatching on the sill. Moreover, this etching should be compared with the Bol portrait of Flinck in the Old Pinacothek, Munich. The position is reversed, the hat and its slant the same, the same effect of robe. And are not the models the same allowing for difference in time, light, and mediums? No doubt I shall be informed that this is Bol following Rembrandt's etching, but Bol did a number of these stone-sill poses, both in etching and in painting. (See V. D., *Rembrandt*, Plate VIII, 29.) Reworked in third state.

OLD MAN WITH DIVIDED CAP, 1640
Hind, 170.

The same hand is apparent here as in the St. Catherine (Hind, 154) listed above. Note a similar stroke in hair, shading of costume, and hatching of background. Note also the Bol hand. These etchings are all dated at a time when Bol was a factotum in the Rembrandt shop.

THE ANGEL LEAVING TOBIAS AND FAMILY
Hind, 185.

A variation of Bol's picture of the Angel Leaving Tobias (given to Rembrandt) in the Louvre. Here is the Bol scratching and scribbling with the cobweb background. Also his types, poses, donkey, and dog. Note the dog for his identity with the dog in the Bol drawing Expulsion of Hagar and Ishmael (Bell, Plate XXIII). Mr. Hind and M. Coppier note that Bol's Gideon's Sacrifice, an etching listed above under Bol, has the figure of Tobias in this etching in reverse. To some this indicates Bol following Rembrandt, but it is singular how like the whole plate to Bol and how little like to Rembrandt. We shall have to give it to Bol. See the drawing for it reproduced in this volume.

VIRGIN WITH INSTRUMENTS OF PASSION
Hind, 193.

The first state of a plate that seems to be after some Italian picture —Mr. Hind suggests a Titian. The etching work suggests Bol. Attribution tentative.

RAISING OF LAZARUS. (THE SMALL PLATE, 1642.)
Hind, 198.

This is a puzzling etching. The composition suggests Horst, the figures indicate Lievens and Bol, the workmanship, especially in the scribbled cobweb background, points to Bol. If the date is correct, all three of them had then left the Rembrandt shop. But the chances are the plate had long been in the shop, and not thought worthy of putting on the market until 1642, when it was resurrected, perhaps reworked, signed, and dated. The Raising of Lazarus theme seems to have originated with Lievens and his etching of 1630. The first drawing for it is in the British Museum, under the name of Rembrandt (Hind, B. M., 2, p. 15). The next Lazarus endeavor in the shop seems to have been the rather immature picture formerly in the Yerkes Collection but now in trade in Paris. This picture I gave to Horst with a query in my Rembrandt book on the paintings. He was in the Rembrandt shop early in the 1630's, and probably knew and was influenced by Lievens as well as Rembrandt. Before he left the shop Bol probably arrived, and out of the Lievens-Horst initiative came the so-called Rembrandt etching of the Resurrection (Hind, 198), in which Bol probably had a working hand. The last phase apparently is the large Resurrection, of later date than 1632 (Hind, 96), in which Rembrandt himself probably recreated the design. The feeling of space and light, the lift of the curtains, the majestic figure of Christ, the dignity and balancing of the composition all speak for a different and greater mind than shows in the earlier Lievens-Horst-Bol efforts. The earlier work is remodelled, redesigned, bettered in every way, and finally put forth as an almost new work. The actual etching of the plate was, no doubt, done in the shop, and several hands worked upon it. Eventually it became a mere Rembrandt shop etching, changed and reprinted through thirteen different states.

*ARTIST DRAWING FROM MODEL
Hind, 231.

The drawing for this etching is in the British Museum (Hind, D., XXVIII), and is listed herein under Bol's drawings given to Rembrandt. The etching is an unfinished experiment but very well done. The scratching of Bol shows all through the foreground. The dark background was probably begun by shop workers and never completed. Compare the model here with the nude figures in the Bol pictures at the Brunswick Gallery—the Candaules, and the Mars and Venus, especially the latter. Haden thought the plate by Bol, and Blanc agrees, saying: "Les travaux au burin qui ont été commencés sur la haute de la planche sont tres probablement de la main d'un élève, de Bol, si l'on veut." (Page 153.)

OLD MAN WITH BEARD
Hind, 350.

Among the Rejected Rembrandt Etchings. Mr. Hind thinks it by Bol, in which conclusion he is probably right.

YOUNG MAN WITH FEATHERS IN HAT

Hind, 358.

> This also is among the Rejected Rembrandt Etchings, and is probably by Bol. Note the spider-web background.

LAMBERT DOOMER
1623?–1700

Doomer was probably a pupil of Rembrandt between 1640 and 1645, a man who did landscapes, animals, and small *genre*. He was not an important factor in the work of the Rembrandt school. Very few of his pictures exist, and though there are a good many drawings by him in Paris, Rotterdam, Amsterdam, London, they lead nowhere in determining Rembrandt problems. Only occasionally are his drawings under Rembrandt's name. The instances that I have noted are the Study of a Pig and of Two Camel Heads, which I have listed below. Rovinski assigns an etching (No. 59) of Camels to Doomer, but the plate is poor and of no importance in Rembrandt study.

DRAWINGS BY DOOMER GIVEN TO REMBRANDT

AMSTERDAM:
RYKS MUSEUM

GOAT'S HEAD

A 3389; Kleinmann, Series I, 53.

> Assigned to the Rembrandt school.

BREMEN
KUNSTHALLE

TWO CAMELS

> Assigned to the Rembrandt school.

DRESDEN
MUSEUM

TWO CAMEL HEADS

Lilienfeld, 84.

> Assigned to the Rembrandt school.

LONDON:
BRITISH
MUSEUM

STUDY OF A PIG

Hind, B. M., 42, p. 25.

> Assigned to Rembrandt.

GERARD DOU
1613–1675

Gerard Dou is another pupil of Rembrandt who, for the present, may be dismissed in any consideration of the Rembrandt etchings and drawings. He may have had a hand in the early shop etchings, but I am now unable to trace it. His work was always too small to be seriously confused with Rembrandt, or even with Rembrandt's pupils. There are a few drawings by him in the British Museum, Albertina, the Louvre, and elsewhere. There is a list of etchings given to him in Wurzbach. No one at the moment cares to question them, or even look at them more than casually. They are hardly Rembrandtesque. Thieme-Becker gives Dou no etchings at all. Some of his pictures were formerly confounded with Rembrandt, and occasionally they still appear put down to the master. The recently acquired Rembrandt at the Ryks Museum is perhaps of this character. It is the Prophetess Anne, or, as it is sometimes called, Rembrandt's Mother. The picture has Dou qualities all through, particularly in the small drawing of the face and hands, the pretty color, the rather sweet textures, and the smooth surface.

WILLEM DROST
?–1678

It is not possible at the present time to reconstruct Drost as an etcher. His paintings show that he worked very much in the Rembrandt vein, many of his pictures are probably still functioning as Rembrandts, and it is reasonable to suppose that his etchings followed in course; but there is no positive proof of this. Two etchings are given him in Thieme-Becker by Doctor de Groot, who writes the article—The Painter (Hind, 355 among the Rejected Rembrandts) and the Woman in Spectacles Reading (Hind, 197). Both are questionable. One fails to see any analogy between this work and Drost's paintings, and it would be impossible to establish his method of etching from either of the plates. I seem to see more of the spirit, sentiment, drawing, and lighting of Drost in the etching of Jan Cornelis Sylvius (given to Rembrandt, Hind, 111). It is an unusual etching in its lighting and hatching, and does not belong to Rembrandt; but neither can it be put down to Drost with any great certainty. As an etcher Drost is still in the shadow.

I have never seen any drawings that could be given to Drost with probability. There are none recorded in the various catalogues and dictionaries.

GERBRAND VAN DEN EECKHOUT
1621–1674

Eeckhout was perhaps as faithful to the Rembrandt tradition as any pupil in the school. He was Rembrandt's close friend and follower, a versatile and talented painter, with a facility for assimilating the striking features of other painters that often proves confusing to the would-be expert. He helped himself not only to Rembrandt but to Flinck, Bol, Lievens, and yet always left a stamp of his own upon the product that can be recognized.   He worked in the Rembrandt shop from about 1635 to 1640, and had there for companions Bol, Flinck, Victors, Horst, and others from whom he probably received impulses and influences.   When he quit the shop he, no doubt, left many of his drawings in the Rembrandt portfolios, because they had become part and parcel of the shop belongings.   Just so with the plates which he etched in the shop.   They were shop property and eventually became known as "Rembrandt etchings."   We shall be able to pick out with some certainty a number of his works from the Rembrandt etchings and drawings.

The landscape drawings usually assigned to Eeckhout in the European print-rooms are misleading.   It is not probable that so accomplished a painter could have done such crude and childish performances.   In the Ryks Museum, for example, the landscapes Nos. A303–A307 are not signed, and are given to Eeckhout only by following some misleading precedent.   The landscapes Nos. A313, A315 are not by the same hand as Nos. A303–A307, and No. A2868 in color is different from any and all the others.   The landscape A3691 is signed, and is a drawing of trees and hills, but has no skill or knowledge in it, and is unbelievable as an Eeckhout. His landscapes in his paintings deny these drawings *in toto*.   At the Teyler Museum there are two river scenes given to Eeckhout that are again feeble performances by some poor pupil.   The British Museum has three landscapes, Nos. 4, 5, 6 (Hind, B. M., p. 76), all signed as Eeckhouts, that are of the same weak character.   It is impossible to reconcile such work with Eeckhout's work unless it be attributed to his salad days before he knew the Rembrandt shop.

On the contrary, there are in Boymans Museum, Rotterdam, two drawings of peasant cottages, windmills, and haystacks quite different from the landscapes attributed to Eeckhout elsewhere.   They are not childish, but broad washed sketches, with racy lines of foliage, and good light effects. They are signed with Eeckhout's initials, that may have been added later. It is not possible to say with certainty that these landscapes are by Eeckhout more than the weak, childish affairs spoken of above.   I note their existence to suggest the uncertainty that exists about Eeckhout as a landscapist.

The figure drawings are not much better.   Many of them are lame, blind, and halt.   It is probable that what has been given to Eeckhout is mere "floor stuff"—things left over that could not be placed elsewhere.

DRAWINGS BY EECKHOUT

AMSTERDAM:
RYKS MUSEUM

BOY IN LARGE HAT

A475.

Attribution questionable.

TOBIAS AND ANGEL

A4306.

This is probably a genuine Eeckhout drawing. It is Rembrandt-esque and quite different from the other Eeckhouts at Amsterdam.

CHRIST ON THE MOUNT

A4674.

Freely and well done in the figures of the foreground. The background opens out to buildings and a tower. Very good work in the Rembrandt manner. A signed drawing.

AMSTERDAM:
DUVAL SALE,
1900

A BOY READING

Smooth and rather pretty, but probably by Eeckhout.

BRUNSWICK
MUSEUM

RAISING OF JAIRUS'S DAUGHTER

Somewhat like a drawing of a similar subject in Kaiser-Friedrich Museum, Berlin, there given to Rembrandt (Lilienfeld, Berlin, 45a), but with slightly different drawing. Attribution tentative.

DRESDEN
MUSEUM

TOBIAS AND ANGEL

B252.

PORTRAIT OF A MAN

This drawing is signed, 1644.

HAARLEM:
TEYLER
MUSEUM

SCENE BEFORE A JUDGE

A feeble drawing for Eeckhout.

THE UNFAITHFUL SERVANT

Placed under "Rembrandt school." Attribution doubtful.

LONDON:
BRITISH
MUSEUM

ANGEL APPEARING TO GIDEON

Hind, B. M., 1, p. 75.

With vines over the house. The hands with Eeckhout's short thumbs. Signed and possibly a genuine Eeckhout, but with no great force about it.

PASTORAL SUBJECT

Hind, B. M., 2, p. 75.

There is some doubt of its being by Eeckhout. It is feeble work.

A BULL BEING LED OUT OF THE GATES OF A TOWN

Hind, B. M., 3, p. 75.

Very likely by Eeckhout.

VIENNA:
ALBERTINA

MARCUS CURTIUS DENTATUS

A formal affair, but probably a genuine Eeckhout.

PORTRAIT OF PHILOSOPHER

Academic and weak.

BATHSHEBA AND DAVID

HEAD OF ORIENTAL

It is nearer perhaps to Salomon Koninck than to Eeckhout.

STUDY OF A PRISONER

A FAMILY GROUP

Reproduced in Meder, *Die Handzeichung*, Wien, 1923, p. 465. I have seen only this reproduction, which certainly has an Eeckhout look about it.

DRAWINGS BY EECKHOUT GIVEN TO REMBRANDT

AMSTERDAM:
RYKS MUSEUM

ANGEL IN HOUSE OF TOBIAS

Lilienfeld, Amsterdam, 7; Valentiner, vol. I, 224.

With Eeckhout's types, diagonal shading of wings, and broad, dark outlines shown in objects near or on the floor. In some features it runs near to Bol, and also to the draftsman whom I have listed hereafter under Group A. Attribution tentative.

ANGEL AND TOBIAS

Lilienfeld, Amsterdam, 8; Valentiner, vol. I, 225.

This drawing is closely related in types and grouping to the central group in the painting of the Visitation (given to Rembrandt, K.K.224) which I assigned to Eeckhout. Even the dog is the same in both works. Note the diagonal shading in the door, costumes, wings. Of course all pen draftsmen and etchers use the diagonal line in shading, but Eeckhout's is peculiar in fineness and in value. I shall refer to it often, because he uses it so frequently that it becomes, with him, a mannerism.

SUSANNA AND ELDERS

Lilienfeld, Amsterdam, 11; Valentiner, vol. I, 262.

It is a drawing for the Kaiser-Friedrich Museum, Berlin, painting (given to Rembrandt, K.K.289), which I have assigned to Eeckhout. Note again the shading with diagonal and straight lines. Another drawing for the same picture in the Albertina, Vienna (Meder, 286). Still another important drawing of the same theme in Kaiser-Friedrich Museum, Berlin, not listed in Lilienfeld.

OLD MAN SEATED

Lilienfeld, Amsterdam, 25.

An Eeckhout type and once more diagonal lines of shading, and dark-rimmed outlines, the exaggeration of which is shown in the British Museum drawing (Hind, D., XI) of a Girl Sleeping, listed below.

AMSTERDAM:
FODOR
MUSEUM

THE VISITATION

An excellent drawing in sepia and color.

BERLIN:
KAISER-
FRIEDRICH
MUSEUM

*JACOB'S DREAM

Lilienfeld, Berlin, 10.

This is a first study for the Eeckhout painting at Dresden of Jacob's Dream (Plate IX, 33). Even the matter of the hat back of Jacob's head is carried out in the painting. The shading of the drawing is not only with diagonal lines, but the composition of both drawing and painting is diagonal.

*THE GOOD SAMARITAN

Lilienfeld, Berlin, 52; Valentiner, vol. I, 382.

Compare for composition and types with Eeckhout's picture of Jairus's Daughter in the Kaiser-Friedrich Museum, Berlin (Plate IX, 35), and the drawing for it (Lilienfeld, Berlin, 45a).

OLD MAN SEATED

Lilienfeld, Berlin, 109; Valentiner, vol. I, 96.

This is a sketch for the etching of Abraham Caressing Isaac (given to Rembrandt, Hind, 148). Both sketch and etching are by Eeckhout.

RAISING OF DAUGHTER OF JAIRUS

Lilienfeld, Berlin, 45a.

To be compared with the painting of the same subject by Eeckhout in the Kaiser-Friedrich Museum, Berlin (Plate IX, 35). It is a study for the painting, but reversed in composition. A similar drawing of the same subject in the Brunswick Museum.

SUSANNA AND ELDERS

Reproduced with an article by Ludwig Burchard in *Jahrbuch der Königlich Preussischen Kunstsammlungen*, vol. 33, p. 175. It is a drawing for the Kaiser-Friedrich Museum, Berlin, picture of the same title given to Rembrandt, but assigned in my book on the Rembrandt paintings to Eeckhout. The drawing is in the broad pen manner of Eeckhout, and should be closely compared with the drawing of the Girl Sleeping in the British Museum (Hind, D., 11; Hind, B. M., 97) given to Rembrandt, but also by Eeckhout. This Berlin drawing is signed "Rebrant." See also the drawings of the same subject listed herein under Amsterdam and Vienna.

RUTH AND BOAZ

Lilienfeld, Berlin, 16; Valentiner, vol. I, 147.

Compare for models with Eeckhout's picture of Abraham and Hagar at Munich (Plate X, 37), and also with the etching (given to Rembrandt, Hind, 149) listed hereafter under Eeckhout's etchings given to Rembrandt. Compare the types and models again with the drawings in the Albertina, Vienna (Meder, 743 and 712), listed hereafter under Eeckhout.

BUDAPEST
MUSEUM

MOTHER WITH CHILD AND DOG

Terey, 18.

Probably by Eeckhout.

33. EECKHOUT: PAINTING OF JACOB'S DREAM
Dresden Museum

34. EECKHOUT (GIVEN TO REMBRANDT): DRAWING OF
JACOB'S DREAM
Berlin Museum

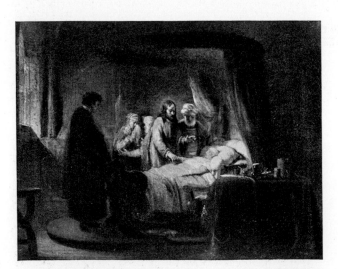

35. EECKHOUT: PAINTING OF RAISING OF JAIRUS'S DAUGHTER
Berlin Museum

36. EECKHOUT (GIVEN TO REMBRANDT): DRAWING OF
GOOD SAMARITAN
Berlin Museum

PLATE IX

37. EECKHOUT: PAINTING OF ABRAHAM CASTING OUT
HAGAR
Old Pinacothek, Munich

38. EECKHOUT (GIVEN TO REMBRANDT): ETCHING
OF ABRAHAM CASTING OUT HAGAR
H. 149

39. EECKHOUT (GIVEN TO REMBRANDT): ETCHING
OF ABRAHAM CARESSING ISAAC
H. 148

40. EECKHOUT (GIVEN TO REMBRANDT): ETCHING OF
ABRAHAM AND ISAAC
H. 214

PLATE X

42. EECKHOUT (GIVEN TO REMBRANDT): DRAWING OF
TOBIAS OPENING THE FISH
Albertina, Vienna

41. EECKHOUT: PAINTING OF TOBIAS OPENING THE
FISH
Brunswick Museum

43. EECKHOUT (GIVEN TO REMBRANDT): ETCHING OF
DEATH OF VIRGIN
H. 161

44. EECKHOUT (GIVEN TO REMBRANDT): ETCHING OF
ANGEL APPEARING TO SHEPHERDS
H. 120

PLATE XI

SUSANNA AND ELDERS
Meder, 286.

Another study for the Kaiser-Friedrich Museum, Berlin, picture of the same subject (given to Rembrandt, K.K.289). Both picture and drawing by Eeckhout. Not reproduced in Terey.

DRESDEN
MUSEUM

YOUNG GIRL AT WINDOW
Lilienfeld, Dresden, 60.

Probably the drawing for the Stockholm picture (K.K.325) assigned in my first Rembrandt book to Eeckhout. The drawing belongs with the painting.

THE HAGUE:
H. DE GROOT
COLLECTION

DEPARTURE OF TOBIAS
Valentiner, vol. I, 227.

I have seen this drawing in reproduction only. It has features such as the types, the lines, and the shading that suggest Eeckhout.

LONDON:
BRITISH
MUSEUM

GIRL SLEEPING
Hind, D., XI; Hind, B. M., 97.

A remarkable brush and wash drawing by Eeckhout, very easily and simply done, but with a striking realization of form. This is Eeckhout's heavy outline carried to the extreme.

LONDON:
OPPENHEIMER
COLLECTION

OLD MAN WITH TURBAN
Valentiner, vol. I, 266.

The same model as in the Kaiser-Friedrich Museum, Berlin, picture of Susanna and the Elders given by me to Eeckhout.

LONDON:
GATHORNE
HARDY
COLLECTION

ANGEL LEAVING TOBIAS
Kleinmann.

MUNICH:
OLD
PINACOTHEK

ANGEL APPEARING TO SHEPHERDS
Neumann, 67.

With Eeckhout's heavy pen line. Composition similar to the Ascension painting here at Munich given to Rembrandt, but by Eeckhout. Assignment tentative.

PARIS:
LOUVRE

OLD MAN SEATED NEAR A BED
No. 22892.

RUTH AND BOAZ
No. 22955.

ZACHARIAS WRITING SON'S NAME
Lippmann, Third Series, 3.

PARIS:
LOUVRE,
BONNAT
COLLECTION

DANIEL'S VISION
Lippmann, 176; Michel, vol. I, p. 20; Valentiner, vol. I, 211.

A study for the Kaiser-Friedrich Museum, Berlin, picture given to Rembrandt (K.K.298), but given in my book on the Rembrandt paintings to Eeckhout. With diagonal lines of shading.

ABRAHAM AND HAGAR
Lippmann, Third Series, 24; Valentiner, vol. I, 15.

TOBIAS AND ANGEL
Lippmann, 183; Valentiner, vol. I, 232.

Reproduced in *Jahrbuch der Königlich Preussischen Kunstsammlungen*, vol. 31, p. 160, with article by Doctor Bode. It is a drawing for the Kaiser-Friedrich Museum, Berlin, picture of the same title given to Rembrandt, but assigned to Eeckhout in my book on the Rembrandt paintings.

PARIS:
  BIBLIOTHÈQUE
  NATIONALE

LOT AND FAMILY
Michel, vol. I, p. 282; Valentiner, vol. I, 39.

PARIS:
  BACHSTITZ
  COLLECTION

SCHOLAR STANDING AT DESK
Formerly in Gallichan Collection, Copenhagen. It is in agreement with Eeckhout's broad pen drawings, particularly the Girl Sleeping in the British Museum (Hind, B. M., 97, and Hind, D., XI).

PRAGUE:
  NOVAK
  COLLECTION

BIBLICAL SCENE
Meder, 1400.

STOCKHOLM
  MUSEUM

PORTRAIT OF GIRL AT WINDOW
Kruse, IV, 2.

PORTRAIT OF GIRL AT WINDOW
Kruse, IV, 3.

VIENNA:
  ALBERTINA

*TOBIAS OPENING THE FISH
Meder, 235; Michel, vol. I, p. 230; Valentiner, vol. I, 239.

This is the drawing for the Eeckhout picture of the same subject now in the Brunswick Museum. The composition is reversed and varied in the picture. Note in the drawing the diagonal lines of shading in the wings, the broad outlines in the foreground and in the foliage. The drawing is in the style of Bol, whom Eeckhout is here probably following.

SEATED FIGURE
Meder, 63.

RUTH AND NAOMI
Meder, 743.

The same models and workmanship as in the Berlin drawing (Valentiner, vol. I, 147).

RUTH AND BOAZ
Meder, 712.

Listed under Rembrandt school. Same model as in Meder, 743, above. The landscape here quite different from those usually assigned to Eeckhout in the European print-rooms.

The Prodigal Son

Meder, 755.

There is a suggestion of Bol in it. Attribution tentative.

Jacob Persuaded to Send Benjamin

Meder, 720.

Attribution tentative.

The Prophet Eli

Meder, 763.

The three drawings above (Meder, Nos. 755, 720, 763) are given to Eeckhout with a question, because they are reminiscent of Bol and Flinck. It may be Eeckhout following them. There are a number of other drawings at Stockholm and elsewhere that might be given to Eeckhout with a query, but the number here given is sufficient to indicate his manner and method.

ETCHINGS BY EECKHOUT

There are some etchings given to Eeckhout by Rovinski, but they seem very doubtful. For Eeckhout's style as an etcher we shall have to depend mainly upon the etchings by him listed below as under Rembrandt's name. A few of them are so unmistakably by Eeckhout in theme, types, composition, drawing, and agree so perfectly with the drawings and paintings that we cannot go far afield in placing them under his name.

AMSTERDAM:
RYKS MUSEUM

Young Man in Cap

An excellent etching and a good illustration of what pupils of Rembrandt could do upon their own initiative. The etching is dated 1646, and is a little more formal and finished than other etchings which I can assign to Eeckhout from the Rembrandt *œuvre*. This is probably owing to the plate having been worked upon by others, either in Eeckhout's shop, or after his death. Two states at Ryks Museum; also one in Fodor Museum (No. 18).

ETCHINGS BY EECKHOUT GIVEN TO REMBRANDT

AMSTERDAM:
RYKS MUSEUM

The Rat-Killer

Hind, 97.

With Eeckhout's type in the doorway, his trees and diagonal composition, his short thumb, and his small, thin lines of shading, sometimes straight, sometimes diagonal, which appear in his pen drawings. In spite of this the actual work on the plate may have been done by some etcher like Van Vliet. Compare closely with the Hind, 148 and 149, listed hereafter. Coppier styles it "travail d'atelier."

*Angel Appearing to the Shepherds

Hind, 120.

The picture, of which the etching is a variation, is in the Louvre, where it is put down, perhaps rightly, to Flinck, though it has Eeckhout earmarks. The etching seems to be some shop performance in which Eeckhout had a hand, notably in the angel and cherubs, the palm-tree, the spot-lighting in the sky and on the ground. Compare it for composition, types, angel wings, cherubs, cloud effects, with the etching Death of the Virgin (Hind, 161), and with the Eeckhout painting Jacob's Dream at Dresden, and the given-to-Rembrandt Ascension at Munich. Put the two paintings and the two etchings side by side in reproduction, and note the similar mind and hand in all of them. The plate (Hind, 120) has been much worried by reworking in dry-point. There are three states, but the first state indicates Eeckhout in its small parallel lines of shading and elsewhere. Assignment tentative.

*Abraham Caressing Isaac

Hind, 148.

There is a drawing (given to Rembrandt) at Berlin (Lilienfeld, 109) for the Abraham in this etching. Both drawing and etching belong to Eeckhout notwithstanding the etching was listed in the inventory of Clement de Jonge (1679), an Amsterdam art dealer, as being a Rembrandt.[1] Compare closely with the title following (Hind, 149) for types, costume, including hats and boots, diagonal composition, the use of the fine line in shading as in Eeckhout's drawings, the short thumb, the spaces of white, notably in the beard and head-dress. This is Eeckhout not only as designer but etcher. The Albertina drawing (Meder, 720), here given to Eeckhout with a query, should be compared. The etching rejected as a Rembrandt by Wilson.

*Abraham Casting Out Hagar

Hind, 149.

A complete presentation of this subject is given in Eeckhout's picture in the Old Pinacothek, Munich. The types in the picture and etching are practically the same, and the Abraham is identical. This again will, no doubt, be declared a case of Eeckhout in the picture following Rembrandt in the etching—the same old threadbare apology. Everything in the etching—types, lines, composition, hatching—declares for Eeckhout and agrees with his work, whereas not one line in it suggests Rembrandt, or agrees with Rembrandt's work. Still, it will be insisted, that no one of the Rembrandt pupils could do anything until Rembrandt had set them a pattern. They were all dummies, seventy-two of them—truly a remarkable collection. Compare this etching with the first that Rembrandt ever did—the Mother of 1628 (Hind, 1)—and see how vastly superior the Rembrandt of 1628 is to this supposed Rembrandt of 1637. Compare the faces closely. Then compare this etching of Abraham with the other pieces here assigned to Eeckhout, and see how it agrees in the way the needle is handled and in the way certain effects of light on the face and elsewhere are produced. Much of the small line-work in the background is drypoint. Haden thought this etching by Eeckhout, retouched by Rembrandt.

*Death of the Virgin

Hind, 161.

Here is Eeckhout with his types, costumes, poses, composition, and studio properties very much in evidence. There are four states of the

[1] De Groot, *Urkunden über Rembrandt*, p. 407.

plate, but Eeckhout shows through them all, especially in the angel and
cherub and sky, done in dry-point.   The Virgin in posture is very like
the Daughter of Jairus at Berlin by Eeckhout; the physician is the
same in both works; the high priest is the Abraham of the etching noted
above (Hind, 149); the man coming through curtains at right is Manas-
seh ben Israel, for whom see the note ahead under Rembrandt etchings
(Hind, 146).   The angel in the etching of the Angel Appearing to
Shepherds (Hind, 120) should be compared with the angel here.   There
can be little doubt about both etchings belonging to Eeckhout.   They
fit in the Eeckhout *œuvre* uncommonly well if they do not belong there.

Virgin and Child in Clouds
Hind, 186.

This is a third etching here listed under Eeckhout (given to Rembrandt) in which the sky and cloud effects are all somewhat similar.
They should be compared with one another.   The line in this last etching is a trifle coarser than the others—probably a bitten line instead
of dry-point.   What a peculiarly Eeckhout hand!   And yet there are
here suggestions of Lievens in the work of the radiating halo and elsewhere.   One state only.

*Abraham and Isaac
Hind, 214.

This is work similar in types, costume, composition, and line to the
two Abraham etchings listed above, with which it should be compared.
It is fumbled and a bit uncertain in the background, probably owing
to reworking by a later hand.   One state only.   Haden thought Rembrandt got the design from Eeckhout, and "so improved upon in his
etching as to make it his own" (p. 27), and Blanc wrote of it: "La
maigreur et la froid du travail, la faiblesse du modelé, le dessin des
jambes, me font penser que l'exécution, du moins, n'est pas de sa
main."   (Vol. I, p. 5.)

Beggars Receiving Alms
Hind, 233.

This is one of the best etchings in the whole Rembrandt *œuvre*, and
yet it is certainly not by Rembrandt, and almost as certainly it is by
Eeckhout.   Here are the types, the composition, the diagonal lines of
shading and the deeply bitten if fine lines of hatching.   Notice the
broad spaces of light on face and back and sleeve and head-dress.
They are peculiar to Eeckhout.   And yet this plate seems suggestive
of Flinck, whom Eeckhout admired and followed.   Practically only
one state—the second state being merely some shading on the door-
post.   Most of the Eeckhouts are one-state etchings.

Jews in Synagogue
Hind, 234.

Eeckhout's types, grouping, and diagonal line-work once more.   It
agrees with many of Eeckhout's smaller and later pictures, and yet
has about it a smack of Aert de Gelder.   It is perhaps a little formal
for Gelder.   Attribution tentative.

CHAPTER VIII

DRAWINGS AND ETCHINGS BY REMBRANDT PUPILS
(CONTINUED)

BERNAERT FABRITIUS
1624–1673

IT is something of a pity that Bernaert Fabritius, one of the most original and forceful of the Rembrandt pupils, should have so little work now left to him under his own name. Recently (1924) there has been brought out to public view, in the Ryks Museum, Amsterdam, three decorative panels by him that were originally painted for a Leyden church. They represent the Prodigal Son, Lazarus and Dives, and the Pharisee, and are remarkable works in their imagination, their lively color, their facile handling. They are very charming panels and show Fabritius in a different phase from his rather sombre if powerful portraits. The more one studies this painter the more he is impressed by his ability and the great wrong that has been done him by considering him as a mere follower of his brother and Eeckhout. He was their equal if not their superior. The pictures still left to him demonstrate as much.

As for his etchings, there is now nothing standing under his name. It is probable that, in common with other painters of his school, he used the etcher's needle, but in the shuffle of time his work has been lost or sold under other names. We cannot now trace his etchings with certainty, lacking a criterion of his technique. His drawings are in the same category. There are a number that may be attributed to him on the basis of his general style, types, and subjects as shown in his paintings, but the attributions must be considered more or less tentative.

DRAWINGS BY BERNAERT FABRITIUS

ROTTERDAM:
BOYMANS
MUSEUM

*PEASANT AND SATYR

A drawing in ink, and red and black chalk, probably the first thought for the Fabritius picture of the same subject in the Bergamo Gallery. There seems little doubt about either the picture or the drawing.

DRAWINGS BY BERNAERT FABRITIUS GIVEN TO REMBRANDT

AMSTERDAM:
RYKS MUSEUM

*JOSEPH'S BROTHERS ASKING FOR BENJAMIN
Lilienfeld, Amsterdam, 4; Valentiner, vol. I, 117.

It presents analogies of types with the Frankfort Fabritius picture the Birth of John the Baptist. Moreover, it shows the favorite composition of Fabritius—a balanced group of figures on an oblong panel. The drawing is pen work all through, and naturally different from the Peasant and Satyr, done in chalk and listed above. Compare for composition with the picture of Peter in House of Cornelius by Fabritius in the Brunswick Gallery.

*CHRIST AND THE DOUBTING THOMAS
Lilienfeld, Amsterdam, 19.

The familiar Fabritius composition on an oblong panel similar to the drawing listed immediately above. It agrees with the London drawing (Valentiner, vol. I, 407) in some features.

THE UNFAITHFUL SERVANT
Lilienfeld, Amsterdam, 16; *Valentiner, vol. I,* 367.

This is the drawing for the painting in the Wallace Museum, London, sometimes called the Centurion Cornelius. In my book on the Rembrandt paintings I assigned this picture tentatively to Simon de Vlieger. My first impression had been that possibly the Wallace Museum painting was by Aert de Gelder—the color, texture, painting, slack drawing, seemed to suggest it—but I could not reconcile this Amsterdam drawing for the picture with the other drawings I was assigning to Gelder. The result was I gave the resemblances suggesting Simon de Vlieger as the possible painter. But I was not satisfied with that attribution (though some of the resemblances were sharp) and added to my note "assignment tentative." I shall now assert my privilege of change by placing the painting to Bernaert Fabritius, but with "assignment tentative" retained in the new attribution. As for the drawing of the Unfaithful Servant at the Ryks Museum, I am also marking that with "attribution tentative." It is nearer the style of Fabritius, especially in its hesitant, broken lines, than any one else in the school. Still it is not identical or absolutely convincing. It has features that suggest Aert de Gelder. A background shows in the drawing at left which is not now apparent in the painting.

AMSTERDAM:
SIX
COLLECTION

HOMER RECITING
Weisbach, Pl. 137.

Attribution tentative.

BAYONNE
MUSEUM

WORKERS IN VINEYARD
Neumann, 69.

There are resemblances here to the Amsterdam drawing of the Unfaithful Servant (Lilienfeld, Amsterdam, 16).

BERLIN:
KAISER-
FRIEDRICH
MUSEUM

CHRIST AND DISCIPLES
Lilienfeld, Berlin, 43; *Valentiner, vol. I,* 361.

With types and models that appear in the drawing, Lilienfeld, Amsterdam, 19, listed above, and also with features that suggest a following of Rembrandt's Supper at Emmaus in the Louvre; *i. e.*, the Christ, the indicated wall space at the back, and the standing figure at left— the same model as the boy carrying in the dish in the Supper at Emmaus. There is a suggestion of Eeckhout in this drawing, as there is in the Rembrandt Supper at Emmaus in the Louvre.

The Last Supper
Lilienfeld, Berlin, 53.

Supposed to have been done by Rembrandt after Leonardo's Last Supper, but probably by the same hand (Fabritius) as the drawings listed above.

Esau Selling His Birthright
Valentiner, vol. I, 58.

The Good Samaritan
Valentiner, vol. I, 373.

Attribution tentative.

FRANKFORT:
STAEDEL
INSTITUTE

*Rest in the Flight
Valentiner, vol. I, 339.

It follows the Moses in the H. de Groot Collection (Valentiner, vol. I, 127) listed below.

THE HAGUE:
H. DE GROOT
COLLECTION

Moses on Mt. Nebo
Valentiner, vol. I, 127.

To be closely compared with the characters in the three panels at the Ryks Museum by Fabritius. The pose and costumes are very much like the Pharisee in one of the three pictures. Note the turned-up shoe and the action of stepping down a step.

Jacob and Joseph's Bloody Coat
Valentiner, vol. I, 98.

I have seen neither of these Hague drawings in the original.

LONDON:
FORMERLY
EARL OF
DALHOUSIE
COLLECTION

Christ and the Adulteress
Valentiner, vol. I, 407.

Probably of Fabritius origin, but not positively so.

LONDON:
FORMERLY
SEYMOUR
HADEN
COLLECTION

Young Man with Long Hair
Michel, vol. 2, 206.

See the note to the etching, Hind, 261, given below to Fabritius with this drawing. Both assignments are tentative.

MUNICH:
OLD
PINACOTHEK

The Doubting Thomas
Neumann, 72.

An earlier and more crowded drawing than the one at Amsterdam (Lilienfeld, Amsterdam, 19; Neumann, 73), but done in substantially the same manner. It is perhaps less carefully done than the Amsterdam drawing, and may be the work of a pupil.

45. B. FABRITIUS: PAINTING OF PEASANT AND SATYR
Bergamo Museum

46. B. FABRITIUS (GIVEN TO REMBRANDT): DRAWING OF
PEASANT AND SATYR
Boymans Museum, Rotterdam

47. B. FABRITIUS (GIVEN TO REMBRANDT): PAINTING OF
TITUS VAN RIJN
Wallace Museum, London

48. B. FABRITIUS (GIVEN TO REMBRANDT): ETCHING
OF TITUS VAN RIJN
H. 261

PLATE XII

49. B. FABRITIUS (GIVEN TO REMBRANDT): DRAWING OF
JOSEPH'S BROTHERS ASKING FOR BENJAMIN
Ryks Museum, Amsterdam

50. B. FABRITIUS (GIVEN TO REMBRANDT): DRAWING OF
JOSEPH'S BROTHERS ASKING FOR BENJAMIN
Louvre Paris

51. B. FABRITIUS (GIVEN TO REMBRANDT): DRAWING OF
REST IN FLIGHT INTO EGYPT
Staedel Institute, Frankfort

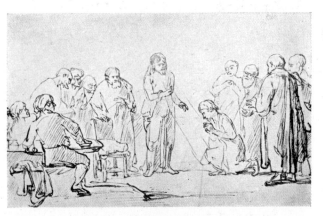

52. B. FABRITIUS (GIVEN TO REMBRANDT): DRAWING OF
CHRIST AND DOUBTING THOMAS
Ryks Museum, Amsterdam

PLATE XIII

PARIS:
LOUVRE,
BONNAT
COLLECTION

*Joseph's Brothers Asking for Benjamin
Valentiner, vol. I, 118.
    By the same hand as the Ryks Museum drawing, Valentiner, vol. I, 117.

Christ Disputing with Doctors
Valentiner, vol. I, 348a.
    Apparently in the style of Fabritius. Attribution tentative.

VIENNA:
ALBERTINA

David Receiving Word of Death of Uriah
Valentiner, vol. I, 162.

ETCHINGS BY BERNAERT FABRITIUS GIVEN TO REMBRANDT

There are no etchings now existent under the name of Bernaert Fabritius. Among the so-called Rembrandt etchings I can find only one that can be given to Fabritius, and the paternity of even that one is doubtful. It is the etching of Titus (Hind, 261)—an etching that stands quite by itself in its manner of execution, and apart from the other work of the Rembrandt *œuvre*. Whether this is the etching-needle of Fabritius or not I am not able to say, having no other authentic etching by him from which to gather his style. The type and theme and sentiment of the etching, however, seem to proclaim its author to be the same person that painted the portraits of the youthful Titus. This person seems none other than Fabritius, though the portraits are all given to Rembrandt, on the probably mistaken supposition that the sitter was his son, Titus. There is no reason to suppose that the sitter was Titus, that tradition being merely an assumption of sentimental historians. None of the painted portraits is in the style of Rembrandt—not even the best of the group, the so-called Titus in the Wallace Museum.

AMSTERDAM:
RYKS MUSEUM

*Titus van Rijn
Hind, 261.
    To be compared with the portraits of Titus in the Metropolitan Museum and Wallace Museum and the children in the Cornelius the Centurion at Brunswick by Fabritius. Also to be compared with any of the so-called Rembrandt etchings for difference in use of needle in outline and shading. There is no certainty about its being a Fabritius etching, but there is certainty about its not being by Rembrandt. Attribution tentative.

CAREL FABRITIUS
1624–1654

Carel Fabritius is more of a myth in his etchings and drawings than in his paintings. There are of his paintings a dozen or more that can be accepted with some certainty, including a new portrait now in the National Gallery, London, but of his etchings nothing remains, and of his drawings nothing that does not require an interrogation-point behind it. I give below two drawings that may possibly be by him. The drawings are evidently both by the one hand: they seem similar in the use of column, steps, pilaster, types, poses, drawing, hands, and in these respects they seem different from any of the drawings in the Rembrandt *œuvre*. They also present some analogies to the Fabritius picture of The Guard at Schwerin and to the general trend of the Fabritius work as seen in his pictures. It must be admitted, however, that this chain of evidence is not too strong, and the drawings given below must be considered more as suggestion than conclusion.

DRAWINGS BY CAREL FABRITIUS GIVEN TO REMBRANDT

STOCKHOLM MUSEUM	JOB AND HIS FRIENDS *Michel, vol. II, p.* 199. Attribution tentative.
VIENNA: ALBERTINA	ST. PETER DELIVERED FROM PRISON *Michel, vol. II, p.* 122. Attribution tentative.

GOVERT FLINCK
1615–1660

The noteworthy thing about the drawings and etchings now left under Flinck's name is that they are, with few exceptions, not Rembrandtesque. He was a pupil of Rembrandt probably as early as 1634, and he signed and dated pictures done in the Rembrandt manner (notably the Isaac Blessing Jacob of 1638) after 1636; but his drawings and etchings of this period seem to have gone into the portfolios of the Rembrandt shop. The drawings now in European museums under his name are, for the most part, later academic work done after he had begun to cultivate classic and semi-aristocratic types, following the Van Dyck formula. It is necessary to repeat that all the pupils of Rembrandt, during their apprenticeship in the shop, did work for the shop, claimed nothing, signed nothing, got nothing. Their pictures were perquisites of the master to be sold for what they would bring, their plates were part of the shop stock in trade, and their drawings were put in the shop portfolios as studio property for the use of workers in the shop. Flinck, Bol, Eeckhout, Gelder—their pupil days with Rembrandt seem barren of result in work. It is only when they left the shop and set up for themselves that their work appeared under their own names. And then only when they developed individual ways of seeing and working that could not be mistaken for those of Rembrandt.

Flinck, one of the brightest and most capable of the pupils, in his early time, did work of much charm and delicacy, and some of his drawings are the most attractive in the Rembrandt *œuvre;* but if he is to be judged by his later blue-paper drawings of academic nonentities, he falls into the commonplace and the negligible. I hope to show that his quality, in both etching and drawing, was at first on a rather high plane. He is now somewhat confused with Bol and Eeckhout, who were with him in the shop. They used the same models and methods, and Eeckhout was a most apt Flinck follower.

DRAWINGS BY FLINCK

AMSTERDAM:
RYKS MUSEUM

HALF NUDE OF WOMAN

A blue-paper chalk drawing in Flinck's flamboyant Van Dyck style. Genuine enough but not representative of Flinck as a Rembrandt pupil.

HAARLEM:
TEYLER
MUSEUM

SYNDIC GROUP

An excellent drawing in red chalk.

LONDON:
BRITISH
MUSEUM

STUDY OF THE NUDE
Hind, B. M., 1, p. 77.

Somewhat elegant, bordering on the pretty.

YOUNG MAN STANDING
Hind, B. M., 2, p. 77.

In the style of Hind, B. M., No. 1, given above.

MAN PLAYING LUTE
Hind, B. M., 3, p. 78.

It is almost like a Watteau, or perhaps Terborch.

LANDSCAPE WITH LARGE TREE
Hind, B. M., 4, p. 78.

I can see nothing of Flinck in this drawing, but, like his other drawings at the British Museum, it is duly signed. Was it the habit then, or now, for artists to sign sketches? Was it not a habit of collectors to sign them for purposes of identification? What proof, then, is the signature? And what other proof in the drawing?

PARIS:
LOUVRE

INTERIOR WITH BED
No. 22948.

It is probably a Flinck. The other Flincks in the Louvre—four sketches of youths and a Shepherd Discovering Nymphs seem quite impossible for him at any stage of his career.

ROTTERDAM:
BOYMANS
MUSEUM

VENUS AND CUPID

YOUTH RECLINING WITH DRAPERY

Both these Rotterdam drawings are in Flinck's later Antwerp manner, and lead nowhere in a Rembrandt inquiry.

VIENNA:
ALBERTINA

MAN'S PORTRAIT

BOY KNEELING

SEWING WOMAN

The three Albertina drawings are again in the pretty Terborch-Van Dyck style, and give no hint of Flinck, the scholar of Rembrandt.

FLINCK'S DRAWINGS GIVEN TO REMBRANDT

AMSTERDAM:
RYKS MUSEUM

*ST. JEROME PRAYING
Lilienfeld, Amsterdam, 20.

Probably a sketch for the etching of St. Jerome of 1632 (Hind, 94), both drawing and etching being by Flinck rather than Rembrandt. Simply and effectively done.

*STANDING WOMAN WITH STICK
Lilienfeld, Amsterdam, 33.

To be compared for pose with the Flinck Diana, a painting in the Liechtenstein Gallery, and also with the Saskia as Flora at Petrograd (K.K.137) given to Rembrandt but by Flinck. The broken line-drawing is unique with Flinck. It is in perfect agreement with that of the St. Jerome listed above.

JACOB BLESSING JOSEPH'S SONS
Valentiner, vol. I, 120.

In the Flinck style but a little lacking in the Flinck spirit and verve. Compare with the Amsterdam picture by Flinck, Isaac Blessing Jacob.

*SLEEPING CHILD
Lilienfeld, Amsterdam, 34; Neumann, 4.

In the manner of the etching by Flinck, listed hereafter, of Woman in Bed. The looped lines and the drawing of the foreshortened face and head are peculiarly like Flinck.

BERLIN:
KAISER-
FRIEDRICH
MUSEUM

STUDY FOR THE HUNDRED GUILDER PRINT
Lilienfeld, Berlin, 45; Valentiner, vol. I, 409.

Under the Flinck etchings given to Rembrandt I shall place the Hundred Guilder plate as being of Flinck's design and partial execution. Here is a study for part of the etching—a pen-and-ink sketch done as mere memorandum for a grouping. It is not accurately done, nor in Flinck's best style. It is done with a coarser pen than usual, and is a little careless in the doing. It may be questioned if by Flinck.

*Saskia
Lilienfeld, Berlin, 89; Hind, D., X.

This is the Flinck type, ideal, pose, sentiment, costume, method, and manner. Compare it with the Amsterdam Standing Woman (Lilienfeld, 33). The inscription is the only reason for thinking it Saskia, and the inscription is a late addition. See the comment upon this on page 6 herein. A beautiful drawing. Compare it with the St. Jerome at Amsterdam (Lilienfeld, 20), and note the scribble at the side in both.

Study of Heads
Valentiner, vol. I, 275.

Note the broken line again—the *Flinck* broken line.

Holy Family
Valentiner, vol. I, 321.

BERLIN:
SCHWABACH
COLLECTION

Study of Model
Valentiner, vol. I, 264.

First study, followed by second study (Valentiner, vol. I, 265), listed below under Paris.

CHATSWORTH:
DUKE OF
DEVONSHIRE
COLLECTION

Isaac Blessing Jacob
Valentiner, vol. I, 64.

A first study for Flinck's picture of the same subject in the Ryks Museum, Amsterdam.

DRESDEN
MUSEUM

Circumcision
Valentiner, vol. I, 306.

In the Flinck manner but apparently by a follower or pupil of Flinck.

THE HAGUE:
H. DE GROOT
COLLECTION

*Christ as the Gardener
Weisbach, Pl. 52; also reproduced in Eisler, "Rembrandt als Landschafter," p. 103.

A first study, perhaps for the Buckingham Palace picture which I assigned to Flinck in my book on the Rembrandt paintings. Compare the broken line-drawing here with that of the Sleeping Child or the Standing Woman (Lilienfeld, Amsterdam, 33 and 34). Another drawing of same subject by the same hand at Dresden (Lilienfeld, 32).

LONDON:
BRITISH
MUSEUM

*Woman in Bed
Hind, B. M., 53, p. 27.

A study for the etching given to Rembrandt (Hind, 163), both sketch and etching being by Flinck. The scribble at the left once more. Other drawings of the same theme at Munich, Paris, and Rotterdam.

Woman in Bed
Hind, B. M., 54, p. 27; Kleinmann, IV, 18.

A study for the etching given to Rembrandt (Hind, 163), both etching and sketch by Flinck. Falsely signed "Renbrant," according to Mr. Hind.

PARIS:
  LOUVRE

FOUR HEADS
Lippmann, 173a.

PARIS:
  LOUVRE,
  BONNAT
  COLLECTION

OLD MAN IN TURBAN
Valentiner, vol. I, 265.

 Compare with Valentiner, vol. I, 264, which is by the same hand, and probably the first attempt.

CHRIST PREACHING
Valentiner, vol. I, 358.

 Probably a tentative sketch for the Hundred Guilder Print, with types like those of Flinck, but done in a manner like Bol, especially the figure of Christ at left.   Perhaps several sketches by different hands were combined in the Hundred Guilder etching.

DAVID ON DEATH-BED
Valentiner, vol. I, 434.

 Possibly by a Flinck pupil or follower.

PARIS:
  ÉCOLE DES
  BEAUX ARTS

RUTH AND NAOMI
Valentiner, vol. I, 433.

 Possibly by a Flinck pupil or follower.

STOCKHOLM
  MUSEUM

WOMAN WITH LARGE HAT
Kruse, IV, 48.

 In red chalk and with less sharpness of edge than if in ink.   Probably a drawing or a following of the Saskia as Flora picture given to Rembrandt, but almost surely by Flinck.

WEIMAR:
  GOETHEHAUS

LOT AND DAUGHTERS
Valentiner, vol. I, 45.

 Possibly by a Flinck pupil or follower.   Doctor de Groot thinks it the drawing for a picture at Budapest by a Rembrandt pupil.

ETCHINGS BY FLINCK GIVEN TO REMBRANDT

LONDON:
  BRITISH
  MUSEUM

*ST. JEROME PRAYING
Hind, 94.

 A drawing for this plate is in the Ryks Museum, Amsterdam, done in the Flinck manner and with his types.   The drawing is more Flinck (even to the little scribble at the side) than the etching, because the etching has been reworked and is now soft in the background.   Even the foreground and the figure have been worn smooth and lack strength in the lines.   Three states.   Haden doubted that Rembrandt did it.

JOSEPH'S COAT BROUGHT TO JACOB
Hind, 104.

 With heads, hands, and attitudes that are somewhat similar to those in the Hundred Guilder Print, and also in the St. Jerome (Hind, 94).   The plate has been attributed to Van Vliet for no particular

53. FLINCK (GIVEN TO REMBRANDT): DRAWING OF ST.
JEROME PRAYING
Ryks Museum, Amsterdam

54. FLINCK (GIVEN TO REMBRANDT): ETCHING OF ST.
JEROME PRAYING
H. 94

55. FLINCK (GIVEN TO REMBRANDT): DRAW-
ING OF STANDING WOMAN WITH STICK
Ryks Museum, Amsterdam

56. FLINCK (GIVEN TO REMBRANDT): DRAWING OF CHRIST
AS THE GARDENER
H. de Groot Collection, The Hague

PLATE XIV

57. FLINCK (GIVEN TO REMBRANDT):
DRAWING OF SASKIA
Berlin Museum

58. FLINCK (GIVEN TO REMBRANDT): ETCHING OF
THREE HEADS OF WOMEN
H. 153

59. FLINCK (GIVEN TO REMBRANDT): DRAWING OF WOMAN
IN BED
British Museum, London

60. FLINCK (GIVEN TO REMBRANDT): DRAWING OF SLEEPING
CHILD
Ryks Museum, Amsterdam

PLATE XV

61. FLINCK (GIVEN TO REMBRANDT): ETCHING OF
REMBRANDT AND SASKIA
H. 144

62. FLINCK (GIVEN TO REMBRANDT): ETCHING
OF HEADS OF WOMEN
H. 152

63. FLINCK (GIVEN TO REMBRANDT): ETCHING OF HEADS
OF SASKIA AND OTHERS
H. 145

64. FLINCK (GIVEN TO REMBRANDT): ETCHING OF
STUDY HEADS AND WOMAN IN BED
H. 163

PLATE XVI

reason. The composition with the peculiar diagonal recession into the background is Flinck's. For this compare with Flinck's Hagar in the Berlin Museum.

*REMBRANDT AND SASKIA
Hind, 144.

The chief figure rather coarsely done; the figure at back seems out of value, but is, in itself, rather well done. The work is in the manner of Flinck, and the long hand is a Flinck convention. To be compared with Three Heads of Women listed hereafter. Coppier thinks the plate a shop piece, and gives it to Bol.

*HEAD OF SASKIA AND OTHERS
Hind, 145.

The same kind of work shows here as in Hind, 144.

*THREE HEADS OF WOMEN
Hind, 152.

Three study heads etched on the one plate in the manner of the plate Hind, 145.

*THREE HEADS OF WOMEN
Hind, 153.

These three heads are in the same manner as those listed above. Compare the Saskia head and hand with the drawing of Saskia (given to Rembrandt) at Berlin (Lilienfeld, 89). It is the same hand at work, even in the scribbling at the side. The plate not signed. Coppier thinks the heads are "studio studies."

*STUDY HEADS AND WOMAN IN BED
Hind, 163.

Drawings for the figures of women in bed are listed above under Flinck's drawings given to Rembrandt (Hind, B. M., 53 and 54). The old woman at the top of the plate appears in hat and feature in the Hundred Guilder Print, as also the man with the tall indented hat. They are all early Flinck types. Plate not signed.

SICK WOMAN
Hind, 196.

To be compared with the etching listed above (Hind, 163), with which it is in agreement. Said to be Saskia ill, but without reason.

THE LUTE-PLAYER
Hind, 200.

In the spirit of Flinck, and much of his method of work still shows at the right and in the foreground; but the plate has been worked over by later hands. The figure at left a little like Bol's Jacob in the Paris drawing (Valentiner, vol. I, 72). Attribution tentative.

HUNDRED GUILDER PRINT
Hind, 236.

Neither date nor signature. The most talked about of all the Rembrandt plates. A very complex composition, designed as an impressive popular etching, but in the working it proved to be quite beyond the designer's powers, and in spite of its qualities of line, light, and shadow, in spite of its characterization and sentiment, it remains something of an experiment. And a puzzle to the connoisseur. There seems little or nothing about it suggestive of Rembrandt's mind or method. He never did such a crowded composition to start with. On the contrary, the grouping, the types, the heads, hats, and hands—especially the hands—the costumes, the draping of scarfs, the poses and attitudes, all point to Flinck as the one who put forth the design. The outline work at the left, where the shadows in costume are only faintly indicated, suggest Flinck's handling of the needle or graver. But several hands have been at work on the plate, and it is impossible to say where one begins and the other leaves off. Through the gloom at the right and the bright light at the left one still sees everywhere the Flinck types and attitudes, slightly varied from his pictures, but still the same in general character. Even the dog is a Flinck dog, just as the young man holding his nose (above the dog) is a Flinck young man, and the man with the high indented hat (above the young man) is a common Flinck property, hat and all. The figures, costumes, faces, models here should be closely compared with Flinck's pictures such as the Abraham Sending Away Hagar at Berlin, the Letter of Uriah at Dresden, the Appearance to the Shepherds, Louvre, Paris, Jacob's Blessing at Amsterdam. Flinck's is really the only hand that can be recognized in this etching. And by way of contrast this print should be placed beside two other etchings given to Rembrandt, the grotesque Entombment (Hind, 281) and the paralyzed Mordecai (Hind, 172). How is it possible that the same hand could do such lame drawing in these two plates and then turn about and do the excellent drawing of the Hundred Guilder Print! But one cannot be too dogmatic about a plate so much to the fore and so universally accepted as by Rembrandt's own hand. The attribution here is tentative.

AERT DE GELDER
1645–1727

After many years of neglect and spoliation Aert de Gelder seems now to be coming into his own. Doctor Schmidt-Degener[1] and Doctor Lilienfeld[2] have written about him, and the latter has given him a liberal assortment of pictures, until now perhaps Gelder has more pictures to his account than he deserves. It is worth noticing that twenty-five pictures given to Gelder by Doctor Lilienfeld are taken from the Rembrandt *œuvre*—that is, they at one time passed under Rembrandt's name, and had, in six cases, his false signature. Gelder is, however, still lacking in well-authenticated drawings. There is a drawing given to him in the British Museum (Adoration of Shepherds, Hind, B. M., 1, p. 78), but it is not in his manner. Nor are the drawings in the Louvre, the Joseph Series (22903–22906), or the drawing (22592) of a sheet of heads any nearer his style. As for his etch-

---

[1] Schmidt-Degener, "Rembrandt du Pecq." im Rotterd. Museum. (In *Zeitschr. f. bild. kunst N. F. XXVII,* 1916.)

[2] Lilienfeld, *A. de Gelder*, Hague, 1914.

ings, there are few, if any, under his name. We shall have to pick out his drawings and etchings in the Rembrandt *œuvre* from their resemblances to his pictures. This is not so difficult to do, for Gelder, though a man of great originality and even genius as regards color, had, nevertheless, his mannerisms and repetitions that mark him apart from others of the school. A love for ornament as such, in head-dresses, veils, fringes, furs, still life, a two-planed composition, architectural effects with many figures, a fancy for Oriental costumes and types, a ploughing, hatching, striating for textural effects, are features of his painting that may be traced with less emphasis perhaps in his drawings and etchings. His dots and spots and hatchings, with both pen and needle, are often quite prominent. Gelder came as one of the late pupils in the Rembrandt shop, and probably was influenced by Van der Pluym, who was then probably in direct charge of the shop. Much work on their different plates seems of common origin as regards style and method.

The drawings and etchings by Gelder as a group should be compared with Bol or Flinck or Eeckhout as a group to get the peculiar personality of each. In mind, emotion, and technique each differs radically from the other. And they are all different from Rembrandt. Putting them under Rembrandt's name and attributing them to his hand is to make a mad confusion of styles. It is almost akin to putting Frans Hals, De Keyser, Mierevelt, and Van der Helst in one *œuvre*. To the man in the street they may all look alike, but not to any one familiar with pictures, drawings, and etchings.

DRAWINGS BY GELDER GIVEN TO REMBRANDT

AMSTERDAM:
RYKS MUSEUM

HAMAN AND ESTHER
Valentiner, vol. I, 202.
Gelder's theme and method. A hasty scribble suggestive of Gelder's picture (given to Rembrandt) belonging to the King of Rumania (K.K.469).

SCENE FROM ESTHER
Lilienfeld, Amsterdam, 23; Valentiner, vol. I, 197.
With suggestions of Bernaert Fabritius here and there.

AMSTERDAM:
F. MÜLLER
COLLECTION

NATHAN AND DAVID
Valentiner, vol. I, 166.
It is Gelder's theme and manner, but apparently at second hand. It has a look of being done after Gelder by some pupil or follower.

AMSTERDAM:
MÜLLER SALE,
JUNE, 1926

MORDECAI AND ESTHER
No. 426.
Washed drawing, giving a different effect from pen work.

AMSTERDAM:
TEIXEIRA DE
MATTOS COL-
LECTION
BERLIN:
KAISER-
FRIEDRICH
MUSEUM

STUDY OF HEADS

Lippmann, Third Series, 89.

*NATHAN AND DAVID

Lilienfeld, Berlin, 18; Valentiner, vol. I, 167.

A good illustration of Gelder's broken line, with his spot-and-dot drawing which is effective by suggestion. Another version of this theme in the former Seymour Haden Collection, and now in the Morgan Library, New York (Valentiner, vol. I, 168).

*HAMAN BEFORE AHASUERUS

Lilienfeld, Berlin, 20; Valentiner, vol. I, 196.

In the manner of the drawing (Lilienfeld, 18) listed above.

*ESTHER, HAMAN, AND AHASUERUS

Lilienfeld, Berlin, 21; Valentiner, vol. I, 201.

The subject is one that Gelder was fond of and treated a number of times. Even some of the Rembrandt authorities think this drawing by Gelder, but it is perhaps less characteristic of him than the two drawings listed immediately above this (Lilienfeld, 18 and 20). An early washed pen drawing, giving a little different look and quality from the ones above. Compare the painting (given to Rembrandt but by Gelder) at Moscow (K.K.453) of the same subject. The types, the composition, the lighting, the baton of Ahasuerus, and even the jug on the table are practically the same in the painting and drawing.

SUSANNA AND ELDERS

Lilienfeld, Berlin, 30; Valentiner, vol. I, 259.

Aert de Gelder was a man of experiments and had a fancy for new effects. His drawing, as his painting, is varied. This drawing is somewhat different from the ones listed above, but it seems, in a general way, to have the same characteristics of drawing.

*STANDING WOMAN

Lilienfeld, Berlin, 117.

This drawing requires little argument for its being by Gelder. Its paternity is obvious on its face. Compare for the differences with Flinck's Standing Woman (Lilienfeld, Amsterdam, 33), and for likenesses the Rebecca in the Gelder picture in Gemeente Museum, Brussels.

TWO WOMEN AND MAN DRINKING

Lilienfeld, Berlin, 134.

The head-dresses of the women suggest Gelder, but the drawing is more like Bol or Flinck. Attribution tentative. Signature "Rembrand" pasted on drawing.

GROUP OF STUDIES

Lilienfeld, Berlin, 149; Valentiner, vol. I, 274.

The costumes and head-dresses, with their drawing, are Gelder's.

BERLIN:
AINSLER AND
RUTHARDT
SALE, 1908

ABRAHAM AND ISAAC

This drawing is known to me only in the reproduction, in Sir Robert Witt's Collection, Portman Square, London.

CHATSWORTH:
DEVONSHIRE
COLLECTION

A CHURCH FATHER

Neumann, 50.

LABAN AND LEAH

Michel, vol. 2, 174; Valentiner, vol. I, 76.

This is a case of two drawings or parts of drawings, being brought together on the same sheet.   Only the part at left is by Gelder.

DRESDEN
MUSEUM

CHRIST PRESENTED TO THE PEOPLE

Hind, D., XXXII.

Evidently a study for the platform group in Gelder's early picture Christ Presented to the People at Dresden.   The drawing is early, too, and a little different from the later dot-and-spot drawings such as the Nathan and David at Berlin (Lilienfeld, 18).   It is in red chalk, which makes some difference.

ORIENTAL AND KNEELING SERVANT

Lilienfeld, Dresden, 37.

DRESDEN:
FRIEDRICH
AUGUST II
COLLECTION

JOSEPH CAST INTO THE PIT

Valentiner, vol. I, 91.

Assignment tentative.

FELDSBERG:
LIECHTEN-
STEIN
COLLECTION

THE CONFERENCE

Meder, 418.

THE HAGUE:
H. DE GROOT
COLLECTION

RUTH AND NAOMI

Valentiner, vol. I, 145.

Assignment tentative.   Seen only in reproduction.

STUDIES FOR HEAD OF MORDECAI

Valentiner, vol. I, 203.

THE HAGUE:
VICTOR DE
STEUERS
COLLECTION

KING AT PRAYERS

Kleinmann.

Another version in Berlin Museum (Lilienfeld, Berlin, 71a).   It is reminiscent of Salomon Koninck.

LONDON:
BRITISH
MUSEUM

WOMAN IN CHURCH

Bell, VIII; Hind, B. M., 57, p. 28.

This is probably the Gelder composition and drawing, though slightly varied in method from the Berlin Standing Woman (Lilienfeld, 117) given above.   There is, however, some doubt.   Attribution tentative.

SCENE FROM MACCABEES

Hind, B. M., 16, p. 19.

NEW YORK:
MORGAN
LIBRARY

NATHAN AND DAVID
Valentiner, vol. I, 168.

See the same theme by the same hand in the Kaiser-Friedrich Museum, Berlin (Valentiner, vol. I, 167).

PARIS:
LOUVRE,
BONNAT
COLLECTION

*ESTHER PRESENTED TO AHASUERUS
Valentiner, vol. I, 195.

CHRIST DISPUTING WITH DOCTORS
Valentiner, vol. I, 346.

Compare with the etching, Hind, 162.

STOCKHOLM
MUSEUM

STUDY OF HEADS
Kruse, IV, 18.

VIENNA:
ALBERTINA

ESTHER DENOUNCING HAMAN
Meder, 1069.

Put down to the Rembrandt school.

JUDAH AND THAMAR
Meder, 1243.

JACOB AND RACHEL
Meder, 7; Valentiner, vol. I, 77.

The types are those of Gelder, but the line is varied again. Attribution tentative. Formerly given to Hoogstraten.

VIENNA:
ARTARIA
COLLECTION

THE TAKING OF CHRIST
Meder, 60.

ETCHINGS BY GELDER GIVEN TO REMBRANDT

LONDON:
BRITISH
MUSEUM

*THE SPANISH GIPSY
Hind, 184.

A variation of Gelder's picture Vertumnus and Pomona, which Doctor Lilienfeld doubts as a Gelder. The work on the etching is quite unusual in manner and method among the Rembrandt *œuvre* etchings—that is, quite different from others—and is not unlike Gelder's pen drawings. But it is not possible to say if this etching is directly from his hand. It may be a shop product, and yet would hardly have been so varied from the picture by a shop assistant. It was originally an illustration for a Dutch tragedy founded on Cervantes's *Preciosa*. No date or signature. Attribution tentative.

*CHRIST PRESENTED TO THE PEOPLE
Hind, 271.

It has been said that Rembrandt in this composition is following Lucas van Leyden, but it seems neither a Lucas nor a Rembrandt composition. It is perhaps the varied etching for (or after) Aert de Gelder's picture at Dresden, Christ Presented to the People. The crayon draw-

65. GELDER: PAINTING OF CHRIST PRESENTED TO PEOPLE
Dresden Museum

**66. GELDER (GIVEN TO REMBRANDT): ETCHING OF CHRIST
PRESENTED TO PEOPLE**
H. 271

67. GELDER: PAINTING OF VERTUMNUS AND POMONA
Prague Museum

**68. GELDER (GIVEN TO REMBRANDT): ETCHING OF
SPANISH GIPSY**
H. 184

PLATE XVII

69. GELDER: PAINTING OF ABRAHAM AND ANGELS
Boymans Museum, Rotterdam

70. GELDER (GIVEN TO REMBRANDT): ETCHING OF
ABRAHAM AND ANGELS
H. 286

71. GELDER (GIVEN TO REMBRANDT): DRAWING
OF STANDING WOMAN
Berlin Museum

72. GELDER (GIVEN TO REMBRANDT): ETCHING OF PETER
AND JOHN HEALING THE CRIPPLE
H. 301

PLATE XVIII

73. GELDER (GIVEN TO REMBRANDT): DRAWING OF NATHAN
AND DAVID
Berlin Museum

74. GELDER (GIVEN TO REMBRANDT): DRAWING OF HAMAN
BEFORE AHASUERUS
Berlin Museum

75. GELDER (GIVEN TO REMBRANDT): DRAWING OF ESTHER
PRESENTED TO AHASUERUS
(Bonnat Collection), Louvre, Paris

76. GELDER (GIVEN TO REMBRANDT): DRAWING OF ESTHER
HAMAN, AND AHASUERUS
Berlin Museum

PLATE XIX

ing for part of it is also at Dresden (Hind, D., XXXII). This is probably not Gelder following Rembrandt, but Gelder following his first master, Hoogstraten, and varying himself in all three works as was his privilege, and no doubt his pleasure. The types, costumes, architecture, the large masses of light and dark, the forced whites, are all Gelder's. It may be that the picture was thought a good one for reproduction, and that Gelder did the actual etching of the first state. With the fifth state the foreground figures were cut out and the plate much reworked. Signed after the sixth state with Rembrandt's name and date, 1655. The etching at that time had been turned into a shop etching, and the name and date probably suited the convenience of the shop or the later owner of the plate. Names and dates have been so abominably misused throughout the Rembrandt *œuvre* that they are almost always negligible. But we have no exact criterion for Gelder's etchings, and in its absence it is necessary to make almost all attributions to him tentative.

PRESENTATION IN TEMPLE
Hind, 162.

Follow the likenesses (beginning with the high priest holding the child) to the Abraham in the Abraham and Angels below (Hind, 286). Compare also with the drawing, Valentiner, vol. I, 346.

*ABRAHAM AND ANGELS
Hind, 286.

Both Doctor Lilienfeld and Doctor Schmidt-Degener have noted the analogies and likenesses in this etching to Aert de Gelder's picture of the same subject in Boymans Museum at Rotterdam. This etching is probably Gelder's work with the needle. Note the resemblances here to features in the Spanish Gipsy etching (Hind, 184). Note the cowled head in the doorway and compare with the Gipsy head. Yet the date, if correct (1656), would make Gelder only eleven years old. Either the date or the attribution is wrong—for Doctor Lilienfeld and Doctor Schmidt-Degener as well as for me.

*PETER AND JOHN HEALING THE CRIPPLE
Hind, 301.

The trees in the background here should be compared with those in the Abraham and Angels etching above (Hind, 286). Also the lines in the shadings of both etchings. Compare the round-faced architecture here with that in Gelder's painting the Presentation of Christ at the Dresden Museum.

ABRAHAM'S SACRIFICE
Hind, 283.

Compare the angel here with the angel in Gelder's painting at Boymans Museum, Rotterdam, Abraham and Angels. Note also the drawing of the wings.

CHRIST AND WOMAN OF SAMARIA
Hind, 294.

This etching follows Hind, 283 and 286. Compare the work of the needle in each case. The composition is, perhaps, adapted from Koninck's etching, Hind, 122.

CHRIST AND PARENTS
Hind, 278.

Attribution questionable. If the date 1654 is correct, then Gelder was only nine years old, and could not have done this plate. But we may ignore the date.

CHRIST DISPUTING WITH DOCTORS
Hind, 257.

CHRIST PREACHING
Hind, 256.

Compare with the drawing, Valentiner, vol. I, 346.

SAMUEL VAN HOOGSTRATEN
1627–1678

Hoogstraten's work is not, at the moment, greatly confused with that of Rembrandt. He stood somewhat apart and had enough originality, with a moderate amount of skill, to produce a respectable if not astonishing quality of art. There are a number of pictures standing in his name that seem authentic, some few drawings, and also a number of etchings of more questionable origin.

Some of the etchings appear as illustrations to books by Hoogstraten and others, but it is impossible to say if Hoogstraten etched the plates. Just so with several plates among the Rejected Rembrandts which Mr. Hind and others give to Hoogstraten. There is question about them. The designs may be Hoogstraten, though the etching of the plates be confused with shop work. But certain properties of pictorial design carry through most of the pictures, etchings, and drawings. Architecture, for example, he employed a great deal as a background for figures. He finally became a little too elegant in his architecture, and seemed to outdo his contemporaries in columns, arches, tiled floors, and the like. This feature he never got from Rembrandt. It is almost impossible to think of Rembrandt in connection with the architectural background of the etching Christ Presented to the People (Hind, 271). I have put the etching tentatively under Gelder's name, but not without a feeling that Hoogstraten, who was Gelder's first master, had a hand or voice in the design. Hoogstraten liked such themes, and probably passed them on to Gelder, who was with him in his formative time, and no doubt got his love of architecture from his master. But as I have said, Hoogstraten's work is not a very important factor at this time in determining the works of the Rembrandt pupils in the *œuvre*, because there seems little of his work there.

CHAPTER IX

DRAWINGS AND ETCHINGS BY REMBRANDT PUPILS
(CONTINUED)

GERRIT WILLEMSZ HORST
1612?–1652

THE story of the utter disappearance of Rembrandt-pupil drawings and etchings is repeated in the case of Horst. One might think that he never sketched or etched, and as for painting that he took up the brush very rarely, because there is given him by the authorities only half a dozen or more pictures. And yet Horst was a prominent Rembrandt pupil after 1630 or 1632, and a man of decided imagination and skill. In fact his work was of such quality that it could pass for Rembrandt's, and almost all of it is now incorporated in the Rembrandt *œuvre*.

I am not able to find a drawing or an etching under his name, but I am quite sure about the identity of certain etchings and drawings by him now under the name of Rembrandt. I may add that I have arrived at these identifications by working backward from the pictures. For instance, the etching of Jupiter and Antiope (Hind, 41) is positively the theme, the style, the composition of the Danae and other pictures by Horst. The type of figure, the bed, the hands, and the drawing are also his. In addition I find the plate etched as no other among the Rembrandt etchings, except those given to Horst hereafter. The manner of hatching, toning, spot-lighting is peculiar. By accepting the Jupiter and Antiope as typical of Horst technically, mentally, and æsthetically, I am enabled to put together a dozen plates all done in apparently the same way. These plates I find agree quite perfectly with two dozen or more drawings, and an equal number of paintings, of Horst origin though now under Rembrandt's name. From that I am forced to conclude that all three kinds of work are from the same source, and that the source is Horst himself. There is, of course, some danger of error in this building-up process, but I submit the process and the result for what they are worth.

The drawings by Horst have been considered in the same way as the etchings. The Berlin Museum drawing of Isaac Blessing Jacob (Lilienfeld, 8a) is the first sketch for the Berlin picture by Horst of the same subject (Plate XX, 77). It is not a Rembrandt drawing that Horst copied or followed. There is nothing so wonderful about either drawing or picture that Horst could not have done both. And they are both his subject, composition, and dramatic effect, with nothing of Rembrandt in or about them. They are too lax for Rembrandt. It is a washed drawing, freely done, with broad outlines, and gives us one kind of Horst sketch work. Using it as a criterion of its kind, it is not difficult to discover other drawings, perhaps in other mediums, that correspond with it. Once more the correspondence of the whole group of drawings with the whole group of etchings and paintings by Horst calls for acceptance.

DRAWINGS BY HORST GIVEN TO REMBRANDT

AMSTERDAM:
RYKS MUSEUM

ISAAC BLESSING JACOB
Lilienfeld, Amsterdam, 2; Valentiner, vol. I, 61.

The same theme and treatment as in the drawing (Lilienfeld, Berlin, 8a) listed below. There can be little doubt that both these drawings are by Horst, and the original sketches for the painting of Isaac Blessing Jacob, by Horst, in the Kaiser-Friedrich Museum. Rembrandt had nothing to do with either drawings or painting. Horst repeated the composition several times, notably in the Earl of Brownlow's picture at Belton House (K.K.172), given to Rembrandt, but by Horst.

AMSTERDAM:
SIX COL-
LECTION

MARGARETHE SIX
Neumann, 37.

Notwithstanding the possession of this drawing by the Six descendants and the tradition handed down concerning it, I must ascribe it to Horst, not Rembrandt. The light flooding from the back, the drawing of the curtain and the table-cloth, the shield on the wall, the pretty bust on the pedestal are distinctly Horst's work. Even the little platform is his. It is an excellent drawing—quite good enough for Rembrandt but too rounded in contours, too flowing in drapery, too formal and academic in composition for him. Yet it must be admitted that there is room for doubt here. The drawing has been carried farther than a mere sketch, has, in fact, been finished up, probably by request, and is almost a picture. This confuses rather than helps identity. Attribution tentative.

AMSTERDAM:
F. MÜLLER
COLLECTION,
1910

FINDING OF MOSES
Valentiner, vol. I, 124.

An early drawing, probably by Horst, and suggestive of his early picture (given to Rembrandt) in the Kaiser-Friedrich Museum, Berlin, the Rape of Proserpina. Attribution tentative.

BERLIN:
KAISER-
FRIEDRICH
MUSEUM

ISAAC BLESSING JACOB
Lilienfeld, Berlin, 8a.

This is another drawing of the same composition cited above at Amsterdam (Lilienfeld, Amsterdam, 2). It is said to be a copy of a version in the H. de Groot Collection at The Hague, which I have not seen except in reproduction (Valentiner, vol. I, 62).

Woman in Bed
Lilienfeld, Berlin, 124.

Here once more the familiar bed and curtain with figures and table which appear so frequently in Horst's compositions. A more hasty sketch than those listed above, and with pen and thumb rather than wash, but essentially the same kind of work.

Healing of Tobit
Lilienfeld, Berlin, 28; Valentiner, vol. I, 246.

Compare head and nose of angel here with those of Jacob in the Berlin drawing above (Lilienfeld, Berlin, 8a), also head of old woman at back in both drawings. Also the style of drawing.

BERLIN:
VAN DIEMEN
COLLECTION

Isaac Blessing Jacob
Valentiner, vol. I, 432.

Still another drawing of a favorite subject with Horst. Types and composition and pen work repeated.

DRESDEN
MUSEUM

Standard-Bearer
Not reproduced in Lilienfeld, Dresden.

Probably the drawing for the picture in the Rothschild Collection, which I assigned tentatively to Horst. Said to be a copy *after* the Rothschild picture. Also one in the British Museum (Hind, B. M., 140, p. 49). Attribution tentative.

DRESDEN:
FRIEDRICH
AUGUST II
COLLECTION

*Sarah Leads Hagar to Abraham
Valentiner, vol. I, 14.

The familiar bed scene with curtains, table at left, and the Horst models with upraised hands. The heavy ink lines peculiar to Horst are apparent in almost all his drawings. Another version in the Louvre, Paris.

Banquet of Esther
Valentiner, vol. I, 200a.

A version of a drawing in the Morgan Collection, New York. Probably both of them genuine Horsts, with curtains, tables, columns, and heavy washed-in darks on either side to focus the light in the centre.

THE HAGUE:
H. DE GROOT
COLLECTION

Nude Woman
Lippmann, Third Series, 95.

I have seen this drawing only in reproduction. Attribution tentative.

*Isaac Blessing Jacob
Valentiner, vol. I, 62.

Ahasuerus, Haman, and Mordecai
Valentiner, vol. I, 199.

The same Horst types, composition, focussing of light and heavy ink work. These drawings have merely to be put together on the table to demonstrate their common origin—put together in reproductions, I mean.

*THE CAPTURE OF SAMSON
Valentiner, vol. I, 142.

This is the drawing for the picture (given to Rembrandt) in the Berlin Gallery. In my volume on the Rembrandt paintings I gave this painting to Horst. This drawing is likewise by Horst, with his curtains, table, jug, figures at back, and light effect.

LONDON:
BRITISH
MUSEUM

*WOMAN WITH ARROW
Hind, B. M., 96, p. 39; Hind, D., Pl. XXIX.

Probably the first study for the etching (given to Rembrandt), Hind, 303. The drawing shown in reverse on the plate. The drawing is too feeble and contorted for Rembrandt. The back and the right leg are not even rightly suggested. The etching also lax in drawing notwithstanding the numerous hands that have worked upon it. Originally it was probably done by Horst, as also this washed drawing. Compare the drawing for the pose of the figure with the etching of Diana at the Bath (Hind, 42), which is another Horst.

WOMAN BATHING
Hind, B. M., 9, p. 17; Lippmann, IV, 75.

Probably the original drawing for the etching (given to Rembrandt), Hind, 42. The etching is listed hereafter under Horst's etchings given to Rembrandt.

WOMAN STANDING BY CHAIR
Hind, B. M., 94, p. 38.

WOMAN BENDING FORWARD
Hind, B. M., 95, p. 38.

All three of the above-listed nude studies are probably by Horst, and should be studied in connection with the etchings by Horst to follow, always, of course, making allowance for the drawings being by one hand only, and the etched plates perhaps by more than one.

LÜTZSCHENA:
STERNBURG
COLLECTION

NATHAN REPRIMANDS DAVID
Valentiner, vol. I, 164.

MUNICH:
OLD
PINACOTHEK

DAVID AND BATHSHEBA
Valentiner, vol. I, 173.

Once more the bed composition, with curtains and figures at the back.

NEW YORK:
MORGAN
COLLECTION

BANQUET OF ESTHER
Valentiner, vol. I, 200b.

Said to be the original of the Dresden drawing (Valentiner, vol. I, 200a). There is no very positive indication of one being a copy of the other. Both of them are probably by Horst, or from his shop.

OLDENBURG:
DUKE OF
OLDENBURG'S
COLLECTION

POTIPHAR'S WIFE ACCUSING JOSEPH
Valentiner, vol. I, 106.

The bed composition again with curtains, table, still life. The composition and grotesque figures of the bed suggest the Danae at Petrograd, which is by Horst.

77. HORST: PAINTING OF ISAAC BLESSING JACOB
Berlin Museum

**78. HORST (GIVEN TO REMBRANDT): DRAWING OF ISAAC
BLESSING JACOB**
H. de Groot Collection, The Hague

**79. HORST (GIVEN TO REMBRANDT): PAINTING OF
CAPTURE OF SAMSON**
Berlin Museum

**80. HORST (GIVEN TO REMBRANDT): DRAWING OF CAPTURE
OF SAMSON**
H. de Groot Collection The Hague

PLATE XX

81. HORST (GIVEN TO REMBRANDT): DRAWING OF SARAH
LEADS HAGAR TO ABRAHAM
Dresden Museum

82. HORST (GIVEN TO REMBRANDT): ETCHING OF JUPITER
AND ANTIOPE
H. 44

83. HORST (GIVEN TO REMBRANDT): ETCHING OF DIANA
AT BATH
H. 42

84. HORST (GIVEN TO REMBRANDT): ETCHING OF NUDE
WOMAN SEATED
H. 43

Plate XXI

85. HORST (GIVEN TO REMBRANDT): ETCHING OF WOMAN
AT BATH
H. 297

86. HORST (GIVEN TO REMBRANDT): ETCHING OF WOMAN
HALF DRESSED
H. 296

87. HORST (GIVEN TO REMBRANDT): DRAW-
ING OF WOMAN WITH ARROW
British Museum, London

88. HORST (GIVEN TO REMBRANDT): ETCH-
ING OF WOMAN WITH ARROW
H. 303

PLATE XXII

VIENNA:
ALBERTINA

Repentant Judas

Meder, Neue Folge, 1922, No. 39.

This is probably the first study for the picture (given to Rembrandt) in the Schickler Collection, Paris. Both picture and drawing by Horst —the drawing agreeing with the other drawings given to Horst herein, especially that of the Capture of Samson, Valentiner, vol. I, 142.

ETCHINGS BY HORST GIVEN TO REMBRANDT

AMSTERDAM:
RYKS MUSEUM

*Jupiter and Antiope

Hind, 44.

This is the smaller plate. If the Danae at the Hermitage, Petrograd, is by Horst—and I have insisted that it is in my book on the Rembrandt paintings—then here in this Jupiter and Antiope is a repetition of the motive, the composition, the type. The same bed effect with canopy, pillows, and bed covering over the lower part of the legs, the same disposition and drawing of the figure as regards the legs and the heavy, sagged-down abdomen, the same opening of the curtains at the back, the same attempt at spot-lighting of the figure from the back, the same shadowy figure at the back. Horst seems about the only one of the Rembrandt pupils who did much with the nude, using a Dutch model, and attempting, step by step, to produce a more select form. He is probably responsible for the etchings of the nudes listed below. This Jupiter and Antiope is very likely an early attempt at etching. It is lacking in drawing, in definiteness (especially in the background), in certainty of line. In other words, it has a fumbled and experimental look. The hatching to produce a shadowy aerial envelope is amateurish and ineffective. Rembrandt, who is so certain in his first etching of 1628 (Hind, 1), could never have done such work as this at any time, but Horst, when in the Rembrandt shop, could have done it with just the juvenile needle here indicated. The work on the plate is different from that of any other in the *œuvre*, except the plates listed hereafter. Contrast the type of the nude here shown with the types in the etching of Adam and Eve (Hind, 159).

Jesus Disputing with Doctors

Hind, 20.

This small plate seems even earlier than the Jupiter and Antiope listed above, and even more tentative and uncertain in its doing. The hatching and shading in foreground and background is ineffective, and even the figures lack detachment. The same hand is apparent as in the Jupiter and Antiope. Besides, the composition of the steps, the dramatic figures, the outstretched hand are all features that belong to Horst and show in his paintings. Coppier says the plate is not by Rembrandt because of the poor drawing. I agree.

*Nude Woman Seated

Hind, 43.

The same type of figure, heavy of abdomen and flabby of flesh, as shown in the Antiope. And the same loose, rambling drawing. Notice the similarity between the enlarged right forearms or the badly drawn left hands in this plate and the Antiope (Hind, 44). Also compare the hatchings in the backgrounds and foregrounds of the two plates.   This is a better and probably a later etching than the Antiope.

*DIANA AT BATH
Hind, 42.

The same model as the Antiope, with the same round face, the heavy breasts and abdomen, the awkward legs, the questionable forearm, the badly drawn right arm, the defective right hand.   Notice this mannered right hand in its agreement with the left hand in the Nude Woman and Antiope.   The design is by Horst in all three plates, but this Diana is better worked and more effective in every way.   Horst has here been helped by expert shop workers, not only in the figure but the drapery, and especially the background of foliage.   Generally considered a Rembrandt shop etching.   The head of this model appears in Rovinski (83) among etchings by Lievens.

*WOMAN SEATED HALF DRESSED
Hind, 296.

This is apparently the same model as the Danae in the Hermitage painting (given to Rembrandt, but by Horst), but in the etching the model appears older.   No doubt the etching was done at a later date than the painting.   The design is probably by Horst, but the work was perhaps done in the Rembrandt shop, and any laxities of line or modelling or banalities of type were corrected in the plate.   Effective in its light.   Seven different states and the plate much worried.

*WOMAN AT BATH
Hind, 297.

This is the same model as in Hind, 296, listed above—the Danae type being here more apparent than there.   The form is more select, as later, and the drawing not so lax, notwithstanding the persistence of the mannered right hand and peculiar forefinger.   The work on the plate is probably Horst's only as regards the figure; the ground apparently is by a softer and more cunning hand.   Note the effective lighting of the figure.

WOMAN BATHING HER FEET
Hind, 298.

Again the same model as above (Hind, 297), with Horst's pillow and tassel as in the Danae and other pictures.   The form is still somewhat hard in line, heavy of abdomen, ill drawn in the right leg, clumsy of hip and shoulder, but all told more select than the earlier samples like the Antiope and the Diana.   The work on the plate seems a carry-on from the earlier Antiope—that is, not yet very cunning or effective, but an improvement on the earlier plates.   There is forceful lighting of the figure, once more—more forceful with Horst than with Rembrandt.   Note the hatching on the figure in its likeness to that of the Woman with Arrow (Hind, 303) to follow.

NEGRESS LYING DOWN
Hind, 299.

Done by the same hand that shows in Hind, 298, listed above—the work on the drapery and the cross-hatching of the background being the same. Much worked in the figure—the drawing of the legs, back, shoulders, and head being lost in a fog of small hatchings and dottings. This has probably given rise to the belief that the figure is that of a negress. It is perhaps merely a white model overworked by small hatchings, in an attempt to get a shadowed envelope.

JUPITER AND ANTIOPE
Hind, 302.

This larger plate seems a later attempt at the same theme as shown in the etching (Hind, 44) listed above. Horst was perhaps here following some print of the Louvre Correggio, but doing so with his usual lax drawing in feet, hands, arms, and legs. The work on this plate in its first state is an improvement on the smaller plate, but is still ineffective—in the lower half of Jupiter or the upper half of Antiope, for example. The second state much reworked. Coppier thinks it impossible as a Rembrandt. He is quite right.

*WOMAN WITH ARROW
Hind, 303.

This is usually supposed to be the last of Rembrandt's dated etchings. It may be the latest of the Horsts, but, while now pretending to a more select type and form, it persists in bad drawing to the end. Some dry-point work on the back may mislead one into thinking it well done, but look at the back of the head, the right forearm, the ill-constructed hip and leg, the bad feet. And there is that same heavy, ill-drawn hand as in the earlier nudes by Horst listed above. And here to the last is Horst's familiar composition—a figure on a bed, curtains at the back, between the curtains a head and face peering out, and a sharp spot-lighting of the figure. The plate much worked over. Rembrandt never did such work. But why not Horst? It is not good enough for the master, but is it not bad enough for a pupil?

SALOMON KONINCK
1609–1656

There is no record that Koninck ever worked in the Rembrandt shop, but then many things have happened in art, literature, and life that have never been recorded. He was a pupil of Moeyaert, and was undoubtedly influenced by Lastman, but he early came under the Rembrandt influence, and worked so positively in the Rembrandt manner that it seems probable he was at one time (say, about 1630 and on) a helper in the Rembrandt shop. His pictures have been freely appropriated to Rembrandt, and as for his drawings and etchings, there is nothing left to him that is creditable, and most of it is not even credible. In the natural course of events it would hardly seem possible for the work of so well known an artist to make such an almost complete disappearance. The truth is he came too near to Rembrandt to be allowed to live as a separate personality.

Of his drawings I have never chanced upon more than two or three under his own name, and of his etchings perhaps a dozen poor affairs that came from his circle are still extant in European print-rooms. But under Rembrandt's name I find plenty of drawings and etchings by Koninck. I list some of them below—enough to make a group and indicate a personality. These personalities of pupils or followers or Rembrandt imitators are fundamentally different one from another—and from Rembrandt. It is not necessary to dispute over names. Indicate the separate groups of works by numbers, and still the personalities are there, and apparent to those who care to see them.

But just there comes in a difficulty that has been existent from the beginning. The Rembrandt interests—and by that I mean the collectors, the gallery directors, and the dealers—are concerned only with names and with big names at that. They want Rembrandts, not Konincks or Horsts, or pupils One, Two, or Three. And so the discovery of new Rembrandts among pupil pictures goes on as merrily to-day as ever. It is a sorry year when critics like Doctor Hofstede de Groot or Doctor Abraham Bredius do not bring in a few new ones. Doctor de Groot has recently discovered (in the *Burlington Magazine* for March, 1924) a Saul Arming David which he declares to be an early work of Rembrandt. He points out the various analogies between this picture and the Goudstikker Young David with the Head of Goliath. And at the end he adds: "It is peculiar that much in this picture goes back more to Nicolaes Moeyaert than to Rembrandt's master, Pieter Lastman." The really peculiar thing is that Doctor de Groot will not see that the Goudstikker Young David with the Head of Goliath is not a Rembrandt, but an oil sketch by Salomon Koninck, and that his newly discovered Saul Arming David "goes back more to Nicolaes Moeyaert than to Rembrandt" because it was painted, not by Rembrandt, but by Salomon Koninck, who was a pupil of Moeyaert, with all that that implies.

Doctor Bredius is also driving on in his discovery of Rembrandts in pictures by Koninck and other pupils. A recently published Baptism of the Eunuch (*Burlington Magazine*, October, 1924), with the telltale tags of Koninck about it, he declares to be an early example of the great master following Moeyaert. Another landscape or two are at the same time given to the master for good measure. Earlier in the year (*Gazette des Beaux Arts*, May (?), 1924) he discovered the supposed mangled original by Rembrandt of Judas Returning the Pieces of Silver, and then straightway declared the Preyer picture of the same subject, formerly in the Schickler Collection, Paris, a mere copy. My suggestion that the Preyer picture is an original Horst did not meet with approval.

DRAWINGS BY SALOMON KONINCK GIVEN TO
REMBRANDT OR OTHERS

AMSTERDAM:
RYKS MUSEUM

MAN IN TURBAN
N. N.

Placed under the Rembrandt school but almost certainly a sketch by Salomon Koninck.

AMSTERDAM:
MÜLLER SALE,
JUNE, 1926

DEPARTURE OF REBECCA
No. 420.

BERLIN:
KAISER-
FRIEDRICH
MUSEUM

*ADORATION OF KINGS
Lilienfeld, 34; Valentiner, vol. I, 299.

In the free sketchy style of Koninck, and with his types, properties, and composition. It is probably the first or second study for Koninck's picture of the same subject in The Hague Museum (Plate XXIII, 89). The central standing king with the turban is the same model in both sketch and picture, the small pages at the back holding up this king's train are the same, and far back is the King from the East, under an oriental umbrella, as in the picture. The Rembrandt authorities will no doubt insist that Rembrandt did the drawing, and Koninck is following it in his picture, but I shall insist there is nothing about the drawing that Koninck could not do, that he varies the composition greatly when he comes to doing the picture, and that the drawing corresponds to Koninck in every way and to Rembrandt in no way.

ESAU AND JACOB
Lilienfeld, Berlin, 11; Valentiner, vol. I, 85.

This is probably Koninck in a very sketchy drawing with a heavier-tipped pen than in the drawings given above.

*THE CIRCUMCISION
Lilienfeld, Berlin, 35; Valentiner, vol. I, 308.

This is probably the first drawing for the etching given to Rembrandt (Hind, 19) which I have given to Koninck. In the etching Koninck appears quite positively not only in the top figure at the table but in the kneeling priest and the pages holding up his train. Early work in the style of his master, Moeyaert. Compare also the oil-painting in the Lehman Collection (Paris, K.K.112) for the likeness and type of the high priest. Compare further with the painting in the Mather Collection, Princeton, by Koninck, reproduced herewith. Drawing, etching, and paintings, all of them by Koninck.

PILATE BEFORE THE PEOPLE
Lilienfeld, Berlin, 57a.

A washed drawing with Koninck's types, methods, and materials, but not entirely convincing. Attribution questionable.

MAN IN TURBAN
Lilienfeld, Berlin, 103a.

Wounded Man
Lilienfeld, Berlin, 126; Valentiner, vol. I, 154.

Here we not only have the Koninck dramatic action, types, and costumes, but here is the true Koninck manner of working with the pen. Compare it with Lilienfeld, Berlin, 34.

Man on Horseback Holding Umbrella
No number, except on mat 4081.

BRUNSWICK
MUSEUM

A High Priest Holding Staff
No number.   With people at the back.

DRESDEN
MUSEUM

Judgment of Solomon
Valentiner, vol. I, 175.

In the style of Moeyaert as regards the composition, but with Koninck types and pen drawing.

DRESDEN:
FRIEDRICH
AUGUST II
COLLECTION

Seated Woman
Lilienfeld, Dresden, 114.

A study for the Petrograd portrait in the Hermitage (K.K.250) given to Koninck in my first Rembrandt book (Pl. XXIII).   The sketch is in black coal and is, consequently, rather unusual for Koninck.   The head-dress and face somewhat rubbed.

HAARLEM:
TEYLER
MUSEUM

Head of a King
Kleinmann, Series I, 25.

It is placed under Eeckhout's name, but is by Koninck or Lievens— nearer to Koninck.   It is a study for or after the picture in New York of King David given to Rembrandt (K.K.Supp. 48).

LONDON:
BRITISH
MUSEUM

Unknown Scriptural Subject
Hind, B. M., p. 37, No. 91.

It suggests Koninck in the pose of the warrior with the two pages behind him.   It is, moreover, Koninck's pen work.   But the attribution is tentative.

*Oriental Standing
Hind, B. M., 64, p. 30; Neumann, 10.

The figure has the pose, the swagger, the costume, the type of Koninck.   The pen drawing a little heavier in line than usual.   This is apparently a rather close following of Rembrandt, but the figure appears again, done in the same manner, in the Berlin Adoration of Kings (Lilienfeld, Berlin, 34)—the central figure.

Pilate Washing His Hands
Hind, B. M., 98, p. 39.

Mr. Hind thinks it the first idea for the picture of the same subject in the Metropolitan Museum which I ascribed to Koninck.   It agrees with the Oriental Standing, given above.   But there is question about it, as also about a similar drawing in the Six Collection, Amsterdam (H. de G., 1233).

NORTHWICK
PARK:
SPENCER-
CHURCHILL
COLLECTION

Oriental Scene

90. KONINCK (GIVEN TO REMBRANDT): DRAWING OF
ADORATION OF KINGS
Berlin Museum

89. KONINCK: PAINTING OF ADORATION OF KINGS
The Hague Museum

91. KONINCK (GIVEN TO REMBRANDT): PAINTING OF DAVID
WITH HEAD OF GOLIATH
Goudstikker Collection, Amsterdam

92. KONINCK (GIVEN TO REMBRANDT): DRAWING OF DAVID
AND ABIGAIL
Weimar Museum

PLATE XXIII

93. KONINCK: PAINTING OF CIRCUMCISION
F. J. Mather, Jr., Collection, Princeton

94. KONINCK (GIVEN TO REMBRANDT): ETCHING OF
CIRCUMCISION
H. 19

95. KONINCK (GIVEN TO REMBRANDT): DRAWING OF
ORIENTAL STANDING
British Museum, London

96. KONINCK (GIVEN TO REMBRANDT): ETCHING OF
MAN STANDING IN ORIENTAL COSTUME
H. 93

PLATE XXIV

97. KONINCK (GIVEN TO REMBRANDT): DRAWING OF MAN
ON HORSEBACK
Boymans Museum, Rotterdam

98. KONINCK (GIVEN TO REMBRANDT): ETCHING
OF TURBANED SOLDIER ON HORSEBACK
H. 99

99. KONINCK (GIVEN TO REMBRANDT): ETCHING OF BAPTISM
OF EUNUCH
H. 182

100. KONINCK (GIVEN TO REMBRANDT): ETCHING OF LARGE
LION-HUNT
H. 81

PLATE XXV

NEW YORK: IN TRADE	**ELEAZAR AND REBECCA AT WELL** *Valentiner, vol. I, 52.*

PARIS:
BEURDELEY
COLLECTION

SOLOMON AND QUEEN OF SHEBA

Here are more of Koninck studio properties—the armed men and umbrella, for example.

ROTTERDAM:
BOYMANS
MUSEUM

*MAN ON HORSEBACK
No. 584.

With plumed hat and spear. A slight drawing, and rubbed a little, but of Koninck origin. Compare with the etching, Hind, 99.

VISITATION
Kleinmann, Series VI, 11.

This drawing is placed under the "Rembrandt school." It has Koninck's man on horseback with spear, and the camel, turban, skunk-cabbage properties that are peculiar to his work.

OLD MAN SLEEPING
No. 581.

By the same hand as shown in the drawing in Boymans Museum, No. 584, listed above.

STOCKHOLM
MUSEUM

ORIENTAL STANDING
Kruse, IV, 5.

TURIN:
ROYAL
LIBRARY

ADORATION OF KINGS
Valentiner, vol. I, 300.

Compare the negro king and his attendant under the umbrella with those under the umbrella in the Berlin drawing (Valentiner, vol. I, 299). Here are once more the manner, the matter, the materials of Koninck. This drawing is a first attempt for the Stockholm, Granberg picture (K.K.Supp. 21)—a picture given to Rembrandt, but assigned in my Rembrandt book on the paintings to Koninck.

VIENNA:
ALBERTINA

PHILOSOPHER
Meder, 242.

Attribution tentative.

WEIMAR:
SCHLOSS
MUSEUM

*DAVID AND ABIGAIL
Valentiner, vol. I, 161.

ETCHINGS BY SALOMON KONINCK

AMSTERDAM:
RYKS MUSEUM

OLD MAN IN PROFILE
Signed 1638.

This is a type of a large scratchy etching somewhat like the Rembrandts (by Lievens) published in Hind, 130, 131, 132, 133. A second old man on same sheet in similar style.

Man in Turban

Signed 1638.   *Bartsch*, 69.

This seems different work from the etching listed above, but it may be pupils' work.

LONDON:
BRITISH
MUSEUM

Old Philosopher Cutting Pen

Bartsch, 28.

Ascribed to Bol, but it should be put down to Koninck.

Busts of Old Men

Rovinski, 69, 70, 71, 72.

These etchings (in the Sheepshank Collection) are all probably by Koninck, or done under his supervision, but they represent him inadequately.   They are his inferior pieces.

ETCHINGS BY KONINCK GIVEN TO REMBRANDT

AMSTERDAM:
RYKS MUSEUM

Rembrandt with Broad Nose

Hind, 2.

Somewhat confused and ill drawn by the use perhaps of a double needle.   With hatching on the coat that appears in etchings listed hereafter.

LONDON:
BRITISH
MUSEUM

Rembrandt Bareheaded

Hind, 3.

Like Hind, 2, given above, this is a commonplace etching, and so bad in drawing (note the figure) as to lead one to wonder why it was ever given to Rembrandt.   It is hardly good enough for Koninck.

Rembrandt Bareheaded

Hind, 4.

Large and coarsely etched, but quite typical of Koninck. The model appears in a picture recently discovered as an early Rembrandt by Doctor Hofstede de Groot.   (See reproduction in *Burlington Magazine*, March, 1924.)   The head directly behind the king's sceptre is the one referred to.   The busts given above (Hind, 2 and 3) derive from the same model.   I have stated elsewhere herein that the "early Rembrandt" picture in the *Burlington Magazine*, March, 1924, is, in my opinion, an early Koninck.

Small Lion-Hunt

Hind, 6.

There are three of these lion-hunts and all of them by Koninck. They all have his loose, scratchy work.   Where he wishes dark shadow he hatches with an open basket-work effect.   Notice this on the rump of the fallen horse, and its repetition on the coat in Hind, 2, and again the open-work effect in the etching Hind, 4, where a split pen or double needle has again been used.   The lion-hunts are said to have been influenced by Rubens, in theme and spirit, but they are not wonderful whatever their source.

AMSTERDAM:
RYKS MUSEUM

*THE CIRCUMCISION. (SMALL PLATE.)
Hind, 19.

A small, much-worked-over plate—worked and reworked to get a sharp effect of light. Koninck's figures in the kneeling priest, the pages holding the robe, and the priest at the back. The drawing for this etching is listed above (Berlin, Lilienfeld, 35). Both etching and drawing given to Rembrandt, and neither of them worthy of him. Professor Frank J. Mather, Jr., of Princeton University, has recently called my attention to a small picture in his possession, in my opinion a free oil sketch of this same subject, by Koninck. With Professor Mather's consent I reproduce it herewith (Plate XXIV, 93).

REMBRANDT BAREHEADED
Hind, 30 *and* 31.

Both of these etchings in their types hark back to the head in the supposed early Rembrandt picture published in the *Burlington Magazine*, March, 1924, and referred to above. In method they agree with the etchings, Hind, 2, 3, 4, listed above. The head (Hind, 31) may possibly be by Lievens. It is not unlike the Beggar on a Bank (Hind, 11).

*MAN STANDING IN ORIENTAL COSTUME
Hind, 93.

This is a typical Koninck in the model, the pose, the breadth of figure, the costume, the hand, the stick, the swagger. The indicated pattern of the under coat and cloak, given by curled and twisted lines, is repeated in the Circumcision etching (Hind, 19) listed above.

*TURBANED SOLDIER ON HORSEBACK
Hind, 99.

This man on horseback occurs several times in Koninck's pictures and etchings. The plate is somewhat scratchy and in manner like Bartsch, 137, or Hind, 314, which is placed among the Rejected Rembrandts. The drawing for this etching is in Boymans Museum, Rotterdam, No. 584.

CAVALRY FIGHT
Hind, 100.

In the manner of the lion-hunts or the etching just listed above (Hind, 99).

SHIP OF FORTUNE
Hind, 106.

Much doubted and variously attributed by Middleton and Dutuit. Haden thought it by Bol, but there is apparently no sign of him in the work. It is Koninck's composition—architecture, grouped people, tall monuments, fallen horse, even the skunk-cabbage growth in the foreground. It is a crowded, confused composition, and rather meaningless, even for Koninck. As for the work, look at the open-work hatching of the sail, or the ship's stern, the light hatching of the arches, and the outlining of the columns for Koninck's needle. The dramatic theme with the battle suggested in the background are also features that point to Koninck. Originally a book illustration appearing at Amsterdam in 1634 in Herckman's *Der Zee-Vaert Lof*.

REMBRANDT WITH PLUMED HAT
Hind, 110.

This is just a Koninck model in a Koninck pose with a great breadth to the figure, an ill-drawn arm and hand on a sword, and a fumbled right arm. Compare it with the Man Standing in Oriental Costume (Hind, 93) listed above. It is a second attempt at a similar effect and with just as indifferent a result. The plate was finally cut down to a head and bust in the second state and then reworked.

CHRIST AND WOMAN OF SAMARIA
Hind, 122.

The composition with a diagonal run away into the background is one of Koninck's favorite arrangements. The architecture with the flattened roof at back, the obelisk, the skunk-cabbage in the foreground are his studio properties. In a similar vein to the Berlin Museum picture Preaching of John Baptist (K.K.174) given to Rembrandt but by Koninck. Attribution tentative.

ST. JEROME KNEELING
Hind, 140.

With scratchy hair and basket-work hatching in the robe and floor. And Koninck's pitcher at the back as in Hind, 19.

MAN IN BROAD-BRIMMED HAT
Hind, 158.

Seidlitz thought this etching by Koninck. It has the Koninck spirit even more than his workmanship. Still there is the peculiar basket-work hatching—peculiar in the sense that its exact like does not appear in any of the other etchings of the Rembrandt *œuvre* save those we have here pointed out as belonging to Koninck.

THE SMALL LION-HUNT
Hind, 180.

*THE LARGE LION-HUNT
Hind, 181.

The three lion-hunts stand or fall together. They are by the same hand—the hand that did the Baptism which follows.

*BAPTISM OF THE EUNUCH
Hind, 182.

Almost all the Koninck studio properties are worked into this etching—the man with spear on horseback, the horses, the eunuch with waiting page, the high priest with long beard, the negro at back with the Oriental umbrella, the distant hill with its obelisk, the immediate foreground with its skunk-cabbage. And all of it in the light, open manner of Koninck. It is a typical Koninck etching. Pictures of the same theme, but varied, are in the Oldenburg and Schwerin Collections, both probably emanating from Koninck, as also drawings at Paris and London. And yet it should be noted, even though not adequately explained, that the type of the priest and much of the light foliage at the back suggest work herein assigned to Aert de Gelder. The priest type belongs to Koninck as the older man, and appears in a number of his works. Perhaps Gelder adopted both the type and the manner.

St. Jerome in Dark Chamber
Hind, 201.

More than once Koninck painted this subject, and this etching is probably of his planning, but whether he did the actual work on the plate one cannot say. It may have been done by a shop engraver. There is said to be a drawing for it in the Gay Collection at Paris, but I have not seen the drawing. Not unlike the Philosopher paintings in the Louvre which I assigned to Koninck in my first Rembrandt book.

Student at Table by Candlelight
Hind, 202.

It follows upon the preceding etching, Hind, 201. The plate has been weakened by reworking. Originally a book illustration appearing at Amsterdam in 1654. It is not universally accepted as by Rembrandt.

CHAPTER X

DRAWINGS AND ETCHINGS BY REMBRANDT PUPILS
(CONTINUED)

JAN LIEVENS
1607–1674

THE student searching the portfolios in the European print-rooms for drawings and etchings by Jan Lievens must gather a very mixed impression of that master. He was a year younger than Rembrandt, they were probably together as youths in Leyden, afterward fellow students under Lastman in Amsterdam, and still later fellow workers together at Leyden. Up to about 1632 they were thought to be painters of nearly equal ability. Some there were who rated Lievens as the brighter mind. Huygens (writing in 1631), comparing him with Rembrandt, praised his "sublimity of invention and a certain audacity in ideas and forms." He must have put out not one but many pictures and etchings to have attained such praise from Huygens. But where are those pictures and etchings to-day? There is very little assigned to him, so far as I can discover, before 1634—three years after Huygens wrote about him. He was then living in Antwerp, had changed his style, and was showing the influence of the Antwerp school. But before that, from a very early age (it is said that he was a pupil of Schooten when only eight years old) he had been working at Leyden and Amsterdam. There was perhaps fifteen years' work in the Dutch manner—much of it, no doubt, in the Lastman-Rembrandt manner. What has become of that?

The European print-rooms show a number of bewildering drawings assigned to Lievens. One finds, for example, a ruck of landscapes (at Berlin 9, at Rotterdam 6, at Paris 5, at London, British Museum, 14). These landscapes for the greater part are lacking in knowledge, subtlety, and artistic value. Any second-rate artist could have done them. Jan Lievens never became famous by such crude work as that. Besides, there are landscapes (in the Sacrifice of Isaac at Brunswick and elsewhere) by Lievens which prove conclusively that he was very far from being crude in this branch of painting. Mr. Hind inclines to give the landscapes in the British Museum to Jan Lievens the younger, but they would do no one any great credit.[1]   As for the figure drawings given to him, they are almost all done in his Antwerp style, following the elegance of Van Dyck.   His etchings are in the same category.   There are by him sixty-five etchings catalogued by Bartsch and Claussin, twenty without signature, twenty signed by Wyngaerde, an Antwerp print-dealer and possible etcher, three signed by P. de Baillu, an Antwerp dealer and engraver.   But these were done at Antwerp after 1634 and before 1642.   Nothing of the Amsterdam-Rembrandt period appears, with one or two exceptions.   After 1650 he returned to Amsterdam to do coppers of Ephraim Bonus, Vondel, and others.

One asks again what about the product in painting, drawing, and etching before 1634?   How does it happen to have disappeared?   And how does it happen that after he had left the Rembrandt circle and influence a number of works appear under his own name?   Certainly a right idea of Lievens—fellow pupil with Rembrandt and praised of Huygens—is not obtainable from what is so laboriously given him by the authorities.   And yet a certain type or model, with a certain single figure and pose, and a further peculiar kind of delicate drawing and soft modelling are so characteristic and so common with Lievens that a large number of his works can be put together, gathered from various sources.   He was a productive artist, and some of his works survive to this day, though not infrequently under other names than his own.   We shall find many of his drawings and etchings under Rembrandt's name.   They will be denied, of course, and the Huygens estimate of him pushed aside; but, after all, the Huygens estimate was not far from right.   Lievens, as an etcher at least, was perhaps second to Rembrandt, but he was second to no one else in the school.   Honor to Rembrandt!   But that does not require that dishonor should attach to all his associates, fellow workers, and pupils.   They were men of much ability, and it will be remembered that several of them superseded Rembrandt in public favor.   They could hardly have done that and been the spineless creatures the authorities make them out.

DRAWINGS BY JAN LIEVENS

AMSTERDAM: **PORTRAIT HEADS**
RYKS MUSEUM   There are five of these portrait heads, two of them copies, and all of them measurably characteristic.   The drawings of landscapes given to Lievens in this museum are questionable.

[1] It appears from the inventories published by Doctor A. Bredius (*Künstler-Inventare; Urkunden zur Geschichte der holländischen Kunst*, Haag, 1915) that Lievens painted many landscapes, but they are not to be found under his name to-day.

HAARLEM:
TEYLER
MUSEUM

OLD MAN
Kleinmann, Series I, 16.

Done in red chalk. Lievens not only had a penchant for the old man with sad eyes, flowing beard, and flowing robe, but he liked red chalk to work with and used it frequently in his drawings.

MAN WITH STICK

In his Antwerp manner and very much in the Van Dyck style.

PORTRAIT OF MAN
Signed I L, 1657.

A matter of puffed-up Antwerp elegance.

LONDON:
BRITISH
MUSEUM

PORTRAITS

There are some twenty-eight drawings given to Lievens at the British Museum. The landscapes we need not consider, for whether by Lievens or not they are not important just here. The Portrait heads are for the most part in his late manner. These are the portraits of Matham, Jan de Heem, Daniel Seghers, Huygens, Tromp, Jan de Witt. The portrait of Petrus Scriverius dates probably before 1631, has the Amsterdam manner about it, and is characteristic in model and pose of Lievens in his Rembrandt period.

STUDY FOR THE ETCHING OF ST. FRANCIS
Hind, B. M., 12, *p.* 86.

Quite in the manner of Lievens and probably done before he left Amsterdam.

STUDY OF MAN'S HEAD
Hind, B. M., 11, *p.* 86.

Signed I L. Lievens finished his drawings with much care, and many of his portrait heads were detailed drawings to be sold rather than studio sketches to be worked up into etchings or portraits. However, some of them did do service as guides to larger and more important works in engraving, etching, and painting.

PARIS:
LOUVRE

PORTRAIT OF OLD MAN
No. 22729.

It is a rather poor piece, probably by a Lievens follower.

PORTRAIT OF OLD MAN
No. 27726.

Not in the Rembrandtesque vein.

HEAD OF YOUNG MAN
No number.

It is in black chalk and in Lievens's late manner.

VIENNA:
ALBERTINA

PORTRAIT OF JAN VOS
Meder, 319.

In black chalk, signed with initials.

DRAWINGS BY LIEVENS GIVEN TO REMBRANDT

BERLIN:
KAISER-
FRIEDRICH
MUSEUM

Old Man with Open Book
Lilienfeld, Berlin, 101.

Old Man with Folded Hands
Lilienfeld, Berlin, 102; Neumann, 1.

The two drawings listed above are typical examples of Lievens. He did substantially the same thing—the type, pose, red chalk, and all—many times. The sketches were also copied and imitated by followers of Lievens. Etchings and pictures were done from them. The etchings in Hind, 27 and 28, are merely variations of the head shown in Lilienfeld, Berlin, 102, listed above; and such paintings as St. Paul Writing (K.K.16) or Bearded Old Man (K.K.Supp. 15) or the Apostle Paul (K.K.15) are but repetitions of the same motive and done in the same manner.

BREMEN
KUNSTHALLE

Old Man with Praying Hands

DRESDEN
MUSEUM

*Susanna and the Elders
Lilienfeld, Dresden, 11; Valentiner, vol. I, 260.

Compare with the drawing for the Raising of Lazarus at London (Hind, D., Plate IX). They are both hasty memoranda by Lievens.

Christ Preaching
Lilienfeld, Dresden, 22.

Entombment
Lilienfeld, Dresden, 31.

FRANKFORT:
STAEDEL
INSTITUTE

Study for the Drunken Lot
Valentiner, vol. I, 42.

There is no doubt about this sketch in black chalk being by Lievens. Nor the second or complete study (Valentiner, vol. I, 41) listed below under the British Museum. It was from this drawing that Van Vliet probably produced his etching. The confusion of it has arisen only because certain authorities insist upon giving the drawings to Rembrandt instead of to Lievens, where they belong.

HAARLEM:
TEYLER
MUSEUM

Old Man
Kleinmann, Series I, 1.

The same motive, the same red-chalk effect.

LONDON:
BRITISH
MUSEUM

*Raising of Lazarus
Hind, B. M., 2, p. 15; Hind, D., Pl. IX.

As M. Coppier has pointed out, this is the study by Lievens for his own etching of the Resurrection (Bartsch, 3, Rovinski, 3). It is a slight grouping for mere memorandum, and it is not surprising that the same sheet should have been used a second time for memorandum of an Entombment of Christ. Another sketch, perhaps earlier, at Boymans Museum, Rotterdam (Valentiner, vol. I, 421).

LONDON:
BRITISH
MUSEUM

LOT AND HIS DAUGHTERS

Valentiner, vol. I, 41.

The completed drawing by Lievens, of which the study listed above (Valentiner, vol. I, 42) is merely a first thought or possibly an afterthought.

VIRGIN AND CHILD

Hind, B. M., 17, *p*. 19.

Attribution tentative.

MAN IN HIGH CAP

Hind, B. M., 18, *p*. 19.

The two drawings above are similar in style, but are not certainly by Lievens. There is doubt about them.

PARIS:
LOUVRE

ST. JEROME

No. 22887.

OLD MAN

No. 22885.

OLD MAN

No. 22581.

OLD MAN IN BED

No. 22961.

*OLD MAN

No. 23000.

These Louvre drawings are typical and unmistakable examples of Lievens's red-chalk drawings, done cleanly, carefully, accurately, but not forcefully or imaginatively. One of the drawings served for the etching of the Aged Man of Letters (Hind, 4*) given to Rembrandt, the figure being reversed on the plate. The drawing is reproduced in Michel, vol. I, p. 40.

ROTTERDAM:
BOYMANS
MUSEUM

*RAISING OF LAZARUS

Valentiner, vol. I, 421.

Perhaps an earlier sketch by Lievens is the Raising in the British Museum (Hind, D., IX). In the same manner as the Susanna drawing at Dresden (Valentiner, vol. I, 260) listed above and with which it should be compared.

WEIMAR
MUSEUM

OLD MAN READING

Meder, Handzeichnung, p. 280; Pauli, vol. II, No. 23.

ETCHINGS BY LIEVENS

There are many etchings given to Lievens rightly enough, but the ones listed below will be sufficient to give an idea of his style and quality. Some of the plates carry the name of Wyngaerde, the Antwerp print-dealer.

101. LIEVENS: PAINTING OF AGED MAN
Schwerin Museum

102. LIEVENS (GIVEN TO REMBRANDT): ETCHING OF OLD
MAN SEATED
H. 92

103. LIEVENS (GIVEN TO REMBRANDT): DRAWING OF OLD
MAN STUDYING
Louvre, Paris

104. LIEVENS (GIVEN TO REMBRANDT): ETCHING OF AGED
MAN OF LETTERS
H. 4*

PLATE XXVI

105. LIEVENS (GIVEN TO REMBRANDT): ETCHING OF OLD
MAN WITH FLOWING BEARD
H. 26

106. LIEVENS (GIVEN TO REMBRANDT): DRAWING
OF OLD MAN SEATED
Berlin Museum

107. LIEVENS (GIVEN TO REMBRANDT): ETCHING OF OLD
BEARDED MAN
H. 47

108. LIEVENS (GIVEN TO REMBRANDT): ETCHING OF OLD
MAN SHADING HIS EYES
H. 169

PLATE XXVII

109. LIEVENS: ETCHING OF RAISING OF LAZARUS
Rovinski, 3

**110. LIEVENS (GIVEN TO REMBRANDT): DRAWING
OF RAISING OF LAZARUS**
British Museum, London

**111. LIEVENS (GIVEN TO REMBRANDT): DRAWING OF
RAISING OF LAZARUS**
Boymans Museum, Rotterdam

**112. LIEVENS (GIVEN TO REMBRANDT): DRAWING OF
SUSANNA AND ELDERS**
Dresden Museum

PLATE **XXVIII**

What part in the actual work upon the Lievens plates he or others had can now only be conjectured.   But it must be understood that most of these plates represent Lievens after 1634, when he was out of the Rembrandt circle, and had adopted the very different Antwerp view of art.

LONDON:
BRITISH
MUSEUM

HOLY VIRGIN
Rovinski, 1.
> Signed by both Lievens and Wyngaerde.   In Sheepshank Collection.

ADORATION
Rovinski, 2.
> This seems poor shop work.

*RAISING OF LAZARUS
Rovinski, 3.
> It is Lievens's design beyond question.   Wyngaerde's name appears upon the plate also.   The drawing for it is in the British Museum (Hind, B. M., 2, p. 15), but (I think) is mistakenly given to Rembrandt.   The drawing and the etching are published in Coppier, p. 16.   The etching is a very considerable work, and is regarded as a Lievens masterpiece. Reproduction herein of both drawing and etching.

ST. JOHN EVANGELIST
Rovinski, 4.

ST. JEROME
Rovinski, 5.
> Black and coarse with straggling lines.

ST. FRANCIS
Rovinski, 6.

ST. ANTHONY
Rovinski, 8.

KNEELING MAN
Rovinski, 9.

MERCURY AND ARGUS
Rovinski, 10.

PLAYERS WITH DEATH
Rovinski, 11.

ORIENTAL FIGURE
Rovinski, 12.

BUST OF ORIENTAL
Rovinski, 13.

Portrait of Castiglione
Rovinski, 14.

Heads of Young Men
Rovinski, 15, 16, 17.

Oriental Heads
Rovinski, 18, 20, 21, 34.

Busts of Men
Rovinski, 22, 23, 24, 35.

Busts of Girls
Rovinski, 25, 27.

Bust of Boy
Rovinski, 26.

Busts of Old Men
Rovinski, 28, 29, 32, 33, 35.

Bust of Woman
Rovinski, 30, 37.

Heads
Rovinski, 38–54.

Portrait of Ephraim Bonus
Rovinski, 56.

Portrait of Vondel
Rovinski, 57.

Portrait of Heinsius
Rovinski, 58.

Portrait of Gouter
Rovinski, 59.

    All these portraits were done for frontispiece illustrations.

Four Evangelists
Rovinski, 64, 65.

Old Man
Rovinski, 66.

Portraits of Robert South and Gasparus Strezo
Rovinski, 75a, 76.

ETCHINGS BY LIEVENS GIVEN TO REMBRANDT

AMSTERDAM:
RYKS MUSEUM

*AGED MAN OF LETTERS
Hind, 4. *

The drawing in red chalk for this plate is in the Louvre under the name of Rembrandt. The plate is not signed.

LONDON:
BRITISH
MUSEUM

BEGGAR SEATED ON BANK
Hind, 11.

This and a number of small plates of beggars agree well with plates given to Lievens by Rovinski. It is in accord, for examples, with Hind, 13, 14, 21, 22, which are all probably by Lievens. Some of them (Hind, 21, 22) are the same types that one finds in Rovinski listed under Lievens. The head (Hind, 31) which I have given to Koninck seems in partial agreement with this Beggar plate.

BUST OF MAN WITH HIGH HAT
Hind, 22.

It is probably by Lievens, though it has some features recalling Koninck. The work is careless, a little fumbled, but approximating the Rembrandt manner. "On le trouve imité deux fois dans l'œuvre de Lievens," Blanc, p. 254.

BALD-HEADED MAN
Hind, 23.

With dotted shadow work on the face and coarse hard work on the coat. On back of the British Museum impression is the White Negress among the Rejected Rembrandts and usually assigned to Lievens.

BALD-HEADED MAN
Hind, 24.

A small plate, a little more delicate in workmanship than the plate (Hind, 23) listed above, but in the same vein and of the same subject or model. Generally said to be Rembrandt's father, without much warrant for saying so.

THREE STUDIES OF HEADS
Hind, 25.

Done sketchily, but in the manner of the plate (Hind, 23) listed above.

*OLD MAN WITH FLOWING BEARD
Hind, 26.

OLD MAN WITH FLOWING BEARD
Hind, 27.

OLD MAN WITH FLOWING BEARD
Hind, 28.

The three heads just listed are all of the same model, done by the same hand, in the same way. The Hind, 26, is the best of the three, an excellent etching if somewhat wavering in planes of the forehead.

*Old Men Looking Down
Hind, 47, 48, 49.

These three plates represent the same model—the same old man with a beard that appears so often in Lievens's work. The flowing beards and the lines of the needle to represent them were attractive features to Lievens. He played with them in painting, drawing, and etching. The heads (Hind, 47, 48) are sharply contrasted in their lights and darks, and are effectively presented. There was no better etching among the Rembrandt followers than this.

Bearded Man
Hind, 53.

A plate given to Lievens (Rovinski, 73) shows this same subject in reverse and is put down to Lievens following Rembrandt; but why could it not be just Lievens himself or work from the Lievens shop?

Bald Man Looking Down
Hind, 86.

It is probably a coarse Lievens. Note the repetition of the effect of light and dark contrasted sharply. Mr. Hind thinks it the work of some Rembrandt pupil or imitator, Claussin says it is "médiocre," and Blanc "gros et rude."

*Old Man Seated
Hind, 92.

This is the Lievens model, theme, and manner of treatment as regards the head and hand. The plate has been reworked in the hat and cloak, and possibly this reworking was done in Bol's student days and done by him. The gashes in the cloak and the textural effect should be compared with those in the Great Jewish Bride (Hind, 127), which is almost surely by Bol. I reproduce a Schwerin picture, given to Koninck but by Lievens, for comparison.

Old Bearded Man with High Fur Cap
Hind, 130.

A coarse etching, done with a coarse needle, probably by Lievens. Compare with the third Oriental Head (Hind, 133) or the Old Bearded Man Looking Down (Hind, 47). They all emanated from Lievens, though some are coarser than others, and were possibly copies after Lievens by some pupil or shop assistant.

*Old Man Shading His Eyes
Hind, 169.

The Lievens type, head, hand, and violent contrast of light and dark. The head is coarsely done but with spirit.

Sending Away of Hagar
Hind, 306.

It is among the Rejected Rembrandts, and Mr. Hind thinks rightly that it is by Lievens, though he queries his attribution.

MAN WITH THICK LIPS
Hind, 353.
> Another Rejected Rembrandt that should be properly listed under Lievens.

MAN WITH BEARD
Hind, 369.
> Still another Rejected Rembrandt that belongs to Lievens.

A number of other etchings in the Rembrandt *œuvre* might be assigned to Lievens, but there are enough here to establish an artistic personality, and to show a way of doing things quite different from that of Rembrandt. They should be grouped and compared with the group of etchings by Rembrandt-Lievens placed under and following Rembrandt's etchings.

NICOLAES MAES
1632–1693

The story of Maes corresponds closely to that of Bol or Flinck or Horst, or any other notable pupil of the Rembrandt school. Practically nothing of theirs that is Rembrandtesque, or belongs to their school period, or just after it, now stands in their names. Their earliest dated pictures begin several years after they have left the shop, and usually indicate some departure from Rembrandt's types and methods. The pictures are not then always Rembrandtesque enough to be held for Rembrandts, and so some of them are left under their makers' names.

After leaving the Rembrandt shop Maes slipped away into a smoother surface and more popular theme than he found in the shop, but nevertheless retained a method of handling, a forcing of sharp white against dark, and a gamut of color that he got from Rembrandt. As he grew older he became still more smooth in surface, sweet in color, sentimental in theme. No one could possibly be deceived by these late pictures. They were far removed from Rembrandt. They were popular in their day, but now directors, collectors, dealers do not care for them, and in our study we are not directly concerned with them or their drawings, or the etchings reproduced from them. We are seeking Maes only in his Rembrandtesque phase. A number of drawings have been assigned to him—some of them doubtfully. They will be listed hereafter. Some of the drawings under Rembrandt's name but done by Maes will also be listed.

As for his etchings, I find none under his own name. Several etchings under Rembrandt's name of nude models seem to have been done after drawings by Maes, but whether Maes also did the etchings I am unable to say. The drawings may have served some shop etcher for material long after Maes had passed on. Copper plates are handed down from shop to shop. Some seventy or more so-called Rembrandt plates still survive in the copper in Paris, and could they speak would tell an even stranger story than their surfaces reveal. There is a volume on Maes—*Nicolaes Maes von Wilhelm R. Valentiner*, Berlin and Leipzig, 1924—that should be consulted for its illustrations.

DRAWINGS BY NICOLAES MAES

AMSTERDAM:
RYKS MUSEUM

WOMAN EMBROIDERING
A drawing in red chalk and almost surely by Maes.

BERLIN: KAISER-
FRIEDRICH
MUSEUM

OLD WOMAN SPINNING

CAMBRIDGE:
FITZ-WILLIAM
MUSEUM

MILK-WOMAN
Two sketches of same subject and kind.

LONDON:
BRITISH
MUSEUM

MOTHER AND CHILD
Hind, B. M., 4, p. 91.

The drawing is too poor for Maes and should go to some pupil or follower. I cannot agree with any of the attributions to Maes in the British Museum Catalogue. Numbers 1, 2 (Hind, B. M., p. 90) are Maes only with a query. Number 3, the Adoration of Shepherds, is the original drawing by Van der Pluym for his picture in the Passion series (given to Rembrandt) at Munich. Number 5, The Holy Family, is the Van der Pluym drawing for The Holy Family at Cassel (given to Rembrandt). A comparison of photographs should be made here. It should prove at least that the rather accurate Maes was not responsible for such heavy blundering drawing as is shown in the drawings of The Holy Family and the Adoration.

LONDON:
OPPENHEIMER
COLLECTION

WOMAN AT TABLE
A smooth, soft, red-chalk drawing. The head turned to the side.

LONDON:
SOTHEBY SALE,
FEB., 1921

OLD WOMAN SPINNING

PARIS: LOUVRE

WOMAN EMBROIDERING
No. 23458.

PARIS: LOUVRE,
BONNAT
COLLECTION

OLD WOMAN PRAYING

ROTTERDAM:
BOYMANS
MUSEUM

GIRL EMBROIDERING

VIENNA:
ALBERTINA

OLD WOMAN WITH BOOK
Meder, 707.

OLD WOMAN SPINNING

113. MAES: PAINTING OF PORTRAIT OF WOMAN
Budapest Museum

114. MAES (GIVEN TO REMBRANDT): DRAWING OF WOMAN
READING
Former Heseltine Collection, London

115. MAES (GIVEN TO REMBRANDT): DRAWING OF MODEL
STANDING
British Museum, London

116. MAES (GIVEN TO REMBRANDT): ETCHING
OF NUDES
H. 222

Plate XXIX

117. MAES (GIVEN TO REMBRANDT): DRAWING OF NUDE
MODEL SEATED
Berlin Museum

118. MAES (GIVEN TO REMBRANDT):
ETCHING OF YOUNG MAN SEATED
H. 220

119. MAES (GIVEN TO REMBRANDT):
DRAWING OF BOY WITH STICK
Bayonne Museum

120. MAES (GIVEN TO REMBRANDT): DRAWING
OF BLIND MAN WITH STICK
British Museum, London

PLATE XXX

DRAWINGS BY MAES GIVEN TO REMBRANDT

BAYONNE
MUSEUM

*BOY WITH BOOK AND STICK
Neumann, 6.
 Note the beaded hesitant outline and cramped hands. Compare with Lilienfeld, Berlin, 151. An excellent drawing.

BERLIN:
 KAISER-
 FRIEDRICH
 MUSEUM

WOMAN READING
Lilienfeld, Berlin, 119.
 Ink and wash with a hesitant broken line.

*NUDE MODEL SEATED
Lilienfeld, Berlin, 151.
 The same broken line as in Lilienfeld, Berlin, 119, just listed, but perhaps with more firmness and sureness.

YOUNG MAN SEATED ON BANK
Lilienfeld, Berlin, 152.
 It is less certainly by Maes than the drawing above (Lilienfeld, Berlin, 151), though it has the same broken line. Attribution tentative.

BREMEN:
 KUNSTHALLE

WOMAN WITH BOOK IN LAP
No. 472.
 Probably a sketch for the picture in Hermitage, given to Rembrandt, but by Nicolaes Maes.

DARMSTADT
MUSEUM

STUDY OF DRAPED FIGURE
Meder, 480.

DRESDEN
GALLERY

NUDE BOY HOLDING STAFF
Lilienfeld, Dresden, 57.
 It is probably Maes, but there is some doubt about it.

BOY DRAWING
Lilienfeld, Dresden, 50.

NUDE BACK OF MAN
Lilienfeld, Dresden, 81.

DRESDEN:
 FRIEDRICH
 AUGUST II
 COLLECTION

PORTRAIT STUDY OF OLD MAN
Lilienfeld, Dresden, 112.
 This is the study for the portrait in the Carstanjen Collection, Berlin, given to Rembrandt (K.K.339), but listed in my first Rembrandt book as by Maes. The drawing is with a broad pen and practically no wash, but otherwise precisely in accord with Maes's work.

HAARLEM:
 TEYLER
 MUSEUM

WOMAN SEATED
Kleinmann, Series I, 27.
 Done with red chalk.

LONDON:
  BRITISH
  MUSEUM

*Model Standing
Hind, B. M., 66, p. 30; Bell, Pl. VII.

Another similar sketch in the Albertina, Vienna. Probably these sketches were used in preparing the etching (Hind, 222) given to Rembrandt—the etching probably shop work in part.

*Blind Man Walking with Stick
Hind, B. M., 120, p. 44; Bell, Pl. III.

Here is the beaded line that seems characteristic of Maes at one period. It is a hesitant dot-and-dash line, but effective nevertheless. The drawing is forceful and expressive—one of the best of the series of model studies that Maes seems to have executed.

LONDON:
  SOUTH
  KENSINGTON
  MUSEUM

Nude Man
No. 434.

LONDON:
  FORMER
  HESELTINE
  COLLECTION

*Woman Reading
Michel, vol. II, p. 200; Heseltine, 16.

The drawing for the Maes Portrait of a Woman at Budapest reproduced herein (Plate XXX, 114). Also the model for the Lady Wantage Portrait given to Rembrandt, but by Maes (K.K.497).

MUNICH:
  OLD
  PINACOTHEK

Girl in Red Jacket
Lippmann, Fourth Series, 9.

PARIS:
  BIBLIOTHÈQUE
  NATIONALE

Hagar in Wilderness

Young Man Nude
Michel, vol. II, pp. 4–5.

A study for the etching (H.220).

PARIS:
  LOUVRE

Old Woman Sleeping

Given to Drost, but it is by Maes.

Reclining Nudes
No. 22886.

Two on one sheet. The one at the bottom seems quite certainly by Maes.

STOCKHOLM
  MUSEUM

Sister Titia
Neumann, 35.

With the same character of drawing already noted.

Woman Embroidering
Kruse, III, 1.

VIENNA:
  ALBERTINA

Nude Youth
Meder, 465.

Nude Youth
Meder, 497.

Old Woman Reading
Meder, 707.

ETCHINGS BY NICOLAES MAES GIVEN TO REMBRANDT

The three etchings (given to Rembrandt) that follow have their counterparts in the drawings by Maes. The work of the needle rather complements that of the pen and is not unlike it, the shading or attempts at it are similar in both drawing and etching, and, of course, the general spirit, theme, and point of view are the same. There is little reason to doubt that Maes etched these plates, and yet in the absence of any authenticated etching by Maes we cannot assert that he did. It is just as probable that the studies by Maes were worked up into etchings in the Rembrandt shop after Maes had left the premises. For be it remembered that the Rembrandt shop really was a shop, and carried on and sold things for what they were worth just the same as any other shop. The modern thought that art in the seventeenth century was a sublimated affair, and artists too ethereal to bother about prices, is a mistaken notion. Rembrandt probably bought and sold and haggled over prices like any other merchant of the time.

AMSTERDAM: *STUDIES FROM NUDE
RYKS MUSEUM   *Hind, 220, 221, 222.*

There is a bare possibility that these etchings are nearer to Horst than Maes. There is so little positive knowledge about the etching of either man that we can do no more than list their works with a query. Still, if these nude studies are compared with the nudes of Horst, a decided difference in the method of drawing—the conciseness and precision of the drawing—will be noticed.

CHAPTER XI

DRAWINGS AND ETCHINGS BY REMBRANDT PUPILS
(CONTINUED)

CAREL VAN DER PLUYM
1630–1672

VAN DER PLUYM has been heretofore an unknown quantity in Rembrandt art and literature, but he is now gradually taking form in what I think his true character. He was a man close to Rembrandt, possibly a relative or connection, besides being a native of Rembrandt's town, Leyden. He came into the shop late, but one knows not the exact date; probably about 1650. In 1665 he with Alexander de Koninck were appointed guardians of Rembrandt's son, Titus.[1] Rembrandt died four years later, in 1669, never having come up from poverty. That Van der Pluym was not only the guardian of Titus but the manager under Rembrandt of the shop, there can be little doubt. Too many things, directly traceable to him, come out of the shop after 1650 to leave any question about his being a producing factor in the shop output after that time.

Rembrandt leaned on him, used him, employed his facile hands and fanciful brain. He was an exceedingly capable if mannered workman, and could design, etch, and bite a copper plate, rework an old one, or print a new one, in a very acceptable manner. Pictures he handled quite as easily. He drew in no free or large way. He was always halting or cramped, and his characters were always more or less stiff in their joints, stood badly, had flat profiles. His picture planes were flat, too—his figures usually being huddled into a spot-light in the foreground, while his middle distance and background ran off into mystery and mere paint. But in spite of these defects he managed to make a considerable show of splendor by variegated and warm colors, brilliant textures, and sharply contrasted lights and darks. He had a lively imagination and invented a variety of compositions—some of them being naïve through their awkwardness, and others picturesque through their rambling line.

That he helped himself to the invention and skill of those in the shop,

---

[1] Hofstede de Groot, *Die Urkunden über Rembrandt*, p. 329.

116

that he reworked and remade and renovated and sent out as new many of the Rembrandt etchings, that he was the man of all work, the manager, the buyer, the seller in the Rembrandt shop, is highly probable.   That he sent out little under his own name, because the shop name was a better one to sell under than his own, and that his work was paid for as shop work by Rembrandt is also probable.   But such matters are now largely conjectural. What we actually know is that by Van der Pluym three or four signed pictures are still in existence, that these pictures agree quite exactly with a dozen or more pictures under the name of Rembrandt, that the style and spirit and mentality of the pictures are repeated in a dozen or more so-called Rembrandt etchings, and twice as many so-called Rembrandt drawings.   And there we have Van der Pluym—or at the least as much of him as can be at present obtained.

There are no drawings or etchings now standing under his name, but I here put together the ones now given to others, and leave to the student the placing of these drawings and etchings beside the paintings to make up what I have so often called an artistic personality.   Again, I submit that, facile follower and imitator that he was, his personality was distinctly different from Rembrandt or any other of the school.   His very facility in adapting, combining, making an amalgam, showed an individuality almost equivalent to genius.   Perhaps these very qualities made possible his age-long confusion with Rembrandt, and answer the oft-asked question: "If Rembrandt did not do it, who did?"

There is another painter whose etchings it is possible to confuse with the Van der Pluym etchings—Aert de Gelder.   Gelder was born in 1645, and was in the Rembrandt shop and probably under Van der Pluym as the immediate head of the shop.   Their etchings run close together, and probably indicate the influence of the older man on the younger, though the younger was a far greater artist.   It is very likely that the so-called "black manner" of Rembrandt is merely the black manner of his shop manager, Van der Pluym, and that he taught that black (or brown) manner to all the late pupils, including Aert de Gelder.

DRAWINGS BY VAN DER PLUYM GIVEN TO REMBRANDT

AMSTERDAM: **NATIVITY WITH SHEPHERDS**
RYKS MUSEUM   *Lilienfeld, Amsterdam, 12; Valentiner, vol. I, 293.*

      This seems a characteristic drawing by Van der Pluym, showing, as it does, his rather heavy outline work.   The drawing is largely suggestive and done, no doubt, for the use of pupils or workers in the school. An early sketch perhaps for a subject much used by Van der Pluym. The drawing was formerly given to Renesse.

JUPITER, MERCURY, PHILEMON, AND BAUCIS
Lilienfeld, Amsterdam, 22.

A drawing for the painting of the same subject (K.K.388) which I assigned with a query to Van der Pluym. The drawing should have a query upon it also.

BERLIN:
KAISER-
FRIEDRICH
MUSEUM

*TOBIT AND WIFE WITH GOAT
Lilienfeld, Berlin, 23.

The study, with figures reversed, for the picture in the Berlin Museum given to Rembrandt (K.K.283), but assigned to Van der Pluym in my first Rembrandt book.

PRESENTATION OF CHRIST IN TEMPLE
Lilienfeld, Berlin, 36; Valentiner, vol. I, 314.

The background architecture is like that in the picture given to Rembrandt of Simeon in the Temple at The Hague. The figures are grouped in a similar manner and are similar in type. The drawing shows Van der Pluym in his finer, smoother, prettier manner, as in such pictures as the Simeon, or the London National Gallery picture Woman Taken in Adultery, both of which belong to Van der Pluym. It is probably an early Van der Pluym drawing.

JOSEPH'S DREAM
Lilienfeld, Berlin, 40.

This is the drawing for the Budapest picture of the same subject (K.K.299), which I put down to Van der Pluym in my first book on Rembrandt.

BREMEN:
KUNSTHALLE

CHRIST AND WOMAN IN ADULTERY

There are two sketches for the National Gallery picture (K.K.279) here at Bremen, the first sketch being tentative and the second carried further. One is a washed drawing and the other a red-chalk drawing. The types are the same. Both of the drawings as well as the London painting are by Van der Pluym. Listed at Bremen under the Rembrandt school.

OLD WOMAN READING
Pauli, vol. V, No. 25.

This is a slight drawing possibly done for the painting of the Old Woman with a Book in her Lap in the Frick Collection. Both drawing and painting by Van der Pluym.

DRESDEN
GALLERY

SEVEN FIGURE STUDIES
Lilienfeld, Dresden, 69.

Perhaps a study for figures in the etching the Three Crosses (Hind, 270) given to Rembrandt, but by Van der Pluym.

FRANKFORT:
STAEDEL
INSTITUTE

ADORATION OF KINGS
Valentiner, vol. I, 305.

It has its analogies with the Van der Pluym picture (given to Rembrandt) of the Circumcision belonging to Earl Spencer (K.K.465), and also the Adoration of Shepherds (given to Rembrandt) at Munich (K.K.284).   Both pictures and drawing by Van der Pluym.

LONDON:
BRITISH
MUSEUM

STAR OF THE KINGS
Hind, D., XIX; Hind, B. M., 31, p. 22.

Parts of this sketch were probably used for the etching of the same subject given to Rembrandt (Hind, 254).   Both drawing and etching in the grotesque style of Van der Pluym.   Mr. Hind refers to another drawing of the same kind and subject with Doctor Strauss in Vienna.

HOLY FAMILY
Lippmann, Fourth Series, 74; Hind, B. M., 63, p. 30.

By the same hand as the Berlin drawing given above (Lilienfeld, 40).

HOLY FAMILY
Valentiner, vol. I, 325a.

*ADORATION OF SHEPHERDS
Hind, B. M., 3, p. 90.

The drawing is attributed to Nicolaes Maes, but belongs to Van der Pluym.   It is his drawing for the picture of the Adoration at Munich (K.K.284) given to Rembrandt, but belonging to Van der Pluym.

HOLY FAMILY
Hind, B. M., 5, p. 91.

Attributed to Nicolaes Maes, but it is the drawing for the Holy Family (given to Rembrandt) at Cassel.   Both picture and drawing by Van der Pluym, with a possibility, however, that the drawing was done after the picture rather than before it, and by some pupil.

LONDON:
FORMER
HESELTINE
COLLECTION

PRESENTATION IN TEMPLE
Lippmann, 184; Heseltine, Pl. 3.

The composition is similar to that in the picture of the Woman Taken in Adultery in the National Gallery, London.   The foreground, middle distance, and background are substantially the same.   Both picture and drawing by Van der Pluym.

LONDON:
OPPENHEIMER
COLLECTION

*ADORATION OF SHEPHERDS
Valentiner, vol. I, 294.

This is the drawing for the picture of the same subject in the National Gallery, London (K.K.285), both drawing and picture given to Rembrandt, and both belonging to Van der Pluym.   See V. D., *Rembrandt*, p. 141.

MUNICH:
OLD
PINACOTHEK

CIRCUMCISION
Neumann, 80; Valentiner, vol. I, 309.

The sketch for the picture of the Circumcision in the Brunswick Museum given to Rembrandt, as also this drawing, but both of them by Van der Pluym.

ADORATION OF SHEPHERDS
Valentiner, vol. I, 295.

A tentative sketch for a subject familiar with Van der Pluym.

ADORATION OF KINGS
Valentiner, vol. I, 301.

NEW YORK:
MORGAN
LIBRARY

ADORATION OF SHEPHERDS
Valentiner, vol. I, 297.

Perhaps an early draft for the Munich picture of the Adoration (K.K.284).

PARIS:
LOUVRE,
BONNAT
COLLECTION

HOLY FAMILY
Lippmann, Third Series, 20.

A sketch for the Petrograd picture given to Rembrandt (K.K.281), but by Van der Pluym and agreeing quite perfectly with his other pictures.

PARIS:
BEURDELEY
COLLECTION

ADORATION OF KINGS

A study for the Buckingham Palace picture (K.K.387) given to Rembrandt, but by Van der Pluym, as also this drawing.

ETCHINGS BY VAN DER PLUYM GIVEN TO REMBRANDT

AMSTERDAM:
RYKS MUSEUM

PRESENTATION IN TEMPLE
Hind, 18.

One of the several etchings of the Presentation. This is the smallest, earliest, and weakest of them, with some features that show a following of Koninck rather than Rembrandt. A drawing for this (much modified in the etching) is listed under the Van der Pluym drawings. It was formerly in the Heseltine Collection (Heseltine, Plate 3). Compare the kneeling groups. Compare also with the drawing at Berlin (Valentiner, vol. I, 314).

WOMAN READING
Hind, 113.

With a badly drawn jaw and neck and a form that will not stand analysis. The head seems to be placed on the wrong shoulders. The date upon this plate (1634) and that upon Hind, 18, above (1630) are, of course, too early for Van der Pluym, but for the present we shall reject the dates. Probably an early Van der Pluym. It has his sentiment.

*TRIUMPH OF MORDECAI
Hind, 172.

It is probably an etching designed by Van der Pluym with all its huddled grouping, and etched by him, fumbled with an uncertain needle, and in the end licked into a shape that is rather effective in its very grotesqueness. There is not a line or a sign of Rembrandt in or about it. He never put together such a composition nor was guilty of such drawing. The etching is neither signed nor dated. It was just a shop

121. VAN DER PLUYM (GIVEN TO REMBRANDT): PAINTING
OF TOBIT AND GOAT
Berlin Museum

122. VAN DER PLUYM (GIVEN TO REMBRANDT): DRAWING
OF TOBIT AND GOAT
Berlin Museum

123. VAN DER PLUYM (GIVEN TO REMBRANDT): PAINTING
OF MADONNA AND CHILD
Cassel Museum

124. VAN DER PLUYM (GIVEN TO REMBRANDT): ETCHING
OF MADONNA WITH CAT
H. 275

PLATE XXXI

125. VAN DER PLUYM (GIVEN TO REMBRANDT):
PAINTING OF ADORATION OF SHEPHERDS
Old Pinacothek, Munich

126. VAN DER PLUYM (GIVEN TO MAES): DRAWING
OF ADORATION OF SHEPHERDS
British Museum, London

127. VAN DER PLUYM (GIVEN TO REMBRANDT): PAINTING
OF ADORATION OF SHEPHERDS
National Gallery, London

128. VAN DER PLUYM (GIVEN TO REMBRANDT): DRAWING
OF ADORATION OF SHEPHERDS
Oppenheimer Collection, London

PLATE XXXII

129. VAN DER PLUYM (GIVEN TO REMBRANDT): ETCHING
OF TRIUMPH OF MORDECAI
H. 172

130. VAN DER PLUYM (GIVEN TO REMBRANDT): ETCHING OF
CHRIST CRUCIFIED BETWEEN THIEVES
H. 270

131. VAN DER PLUYM (GIVEN TO REMBRANDT): ETCHING
OF THE ENTOMBMENT
H. 281

132. VAN DER PLUYM (GIVEN TO REMBRANDT):
ETCHING OF PRESENTATION IN TEMPLE
H. 279

PLATE XXXIII

pot-boiler put forth by Van der Pluym as shop director, perhaps with the aid of Aert de Gelder, then a pupil in the shop. It has all the Van der Pluym characteristics in types, costumes, architectural background, awkwardness, confusion, and yet with it a strong contrast of the lights and darks that is effective, prints well, and looks convincing.

CHRIST BETWEEN TWO THIEVES
Hind, 173.

An oval plate designed by Van der Pluym, with a head and shoulders pushed into almost every available space on the plate. It is the characteristic huddled and awkward grouping of Van der Pluym, with his types, costumes, and lighting. The figures have been worked over with a niggling needle and are soft and vapory. Any beauty that may be in the etched line is not here apparent. Rembrandt never did it, and no one ever had the temerity of soul to either sign or date the plate. But Coppier declares it to be one of the plates "les plus parfaites et les plus rares, dans l'ensemble de l'œuvre gravé de Rembrandt."

DESCENT FROM THE CROSS
Hind, 199.

This is the start of an etching. For some reason it was carried no farther. No doubt Van der Pluym thought to add tone and a contrasting dark ground. This early state shows his line-work to advantage, and also shows how he kept adding heads in loopholes in the composition until there was no space left. Note the repeated woman's head at the right and left of the cross. Not the worst of the Van der Pluym etchings given to Rembrandt.

FLIGHT INTO EGYPT
Hind, 253.

Another Van der Pluym night scene with a lantern. With changes in the different states. Much worked upon in the shop, the light concentrated against a black ground in later states.

STAR OF THE KINGS
Hind, 254.

Another Van der Pluym night scene with artificial lighting and a tone effect. The print looks heavy and worried. The plate is neither signed nor dated. All of these plates given to Van der Pluym seem convincingly by one hand, and that hand quite different from every other in the Rembrandt *œuvre*. A drawing for this plate in the British Museum, and here listed under Van der Pluym's drawings given to Rembrandt.

ADORATION OF SHEPHERDS
Hind, 255.

The same artificial lighting and driving of lights against darks. The lantern, types, head-dresses, effect of light, as in the Munich picture of the Adoration (K.K.284) given to Rembrandt, but by Van der Pluym. "Le caractère des têtes, le dessin sans esprit, les figures de Joseph, de la Vierge et de l'Enfant, la nature même du travail, qui est à la fois lourd et mesquin, peuvent faire croire que Rembrandt n'est pas l'auteur de la gravure" (Blanc, p. 22).

David in Prayer
Hind, 258.

A crude etching that was probably started by Van der Pluym and never finished, though it has some features that reflect Aert de Gelder. "Un des plus faibles de l'œuvre," says Blanc. But it is signed as a Rembrandt and dated 1652.

*Christ Crucified Between Thieves
Hind, 270.

The etching usually known as the Three Crosses. There are five states of it. With the fourth state the whole plate is changed to an almost meaningless arrangement in which dark lines like curtains are made to veil the whole scene. This is a Van der Pluym mannerism which will be seen in other etchings given to him. The effect produced is what the connoisseurs have called "tone" and "atmosphere." They regard the plate as a Rembrandt masterpiece. The first state of this etching shows Van der Pluym's crowding of space, his awkwardness (look at the wooden horse), his spot-lighting, violent contrast of the light and dark, his types, his costumes, drawing. The plate in all states prints well, and at the present time with three hundred years of old ink and paper it looks well, but when originally printed its defects must have been very noticeable. The types appearing here and there are not unlike those of Aert de Gelder. He seems to have had a hand in a number of these Van der Pluym plates.

Adoration of Shepherds
Hind, 273.

A variation of a subject which Van der Pluym evidently delighted in for the effect of artificial lighting it gave him. Compare the dark treatment of same subject, Hind, 255.

Circumcision
Hind, 274.

This is a badly drawn and loose-jointed example of Van der Pluym. It is perhaps for that reason signed twice as a Rembrandt. The same motive, sentiment, and types as heretofore. Blanc notes that it is the same style as the Adoration (Hind, 255) and the Madonna with Cat (Hind, 275), both of them assigned herein to Van der Pluym.

*Madonna and Child with Cat
Hind, 275.

The composition is a variation of Van der Pluym's Holy Family at Cassel given to Rembrandt. Coarse, shadowy, and ineffective in the background right and left. The face and hands of the Madonna reinforced, and now out of value.

Flight Into Egypt
Hind, 276.

A coarse and fumbled etching in its first state, with Van der Pluym types and drawing, and also with a sentiment and a feeling that Van der Pluym shows in almost all his work.

*Presentation in Temple
Hind, 279.

This is a Van der Pluym experiment—the carrying out to its last stage of his fancy for forcing light against dark. The lights here are little more than sparkling spots, but the general effect is quite effective. This is probably his masterpiece, though perhaps he did not realize it, for the plate is neither signed nor dated. The effect of brilliancy is almost bizarre. Line-work is hardly thought of, but in its place only the sparkling light, the lift of the figures, the excellent setting. But one keeps returning to the ornate Byzantine quality of it. No other etching in the *œuvre* is quite like it. And it is almost the direct opposite of Rembrandt's way of seeing and working. For, after all, Rembrandt, for a Dutchman, was classic in such portrait groups as the Night Watch, or such single portraits as the Jan Six. But here is something that keeps reminding one of Gothic glass or Byzantine gold work. It is an outrage to take such excellent work from Van der Pluym, and mere confusion to give it to Rembrandt. In the black manner produced by much dry-point work, and suggesting Aert de Gelder as a helper.

Descent from Cross
Hind, 280.

This is a night scene, the light coming from a torch in the centre—the kind of scene that Van der Pluym used in his picture of the Nativity (given to Rembrandt) at Munich. The artificial lighting aided his scheme for driving the light sharply against the dark. The Van der Pluym awkwardness in drawing is here, but the actual work on the plate may have been helped out by shop assistance. It is coarse, violent, but effective work.

*The Entombment
Hind, 281.

The lighting is artificial as in the Descent (Hind, 280) listed above, but with a still more violent central concentration. The first state is entirely line-work; the second state has the ground much darkened, and the effect is almost that of a mezzotint.

CONSTANTIN A. RENESSE
1626–1680

There were a dozen or more pupils of Rembrandt—painters and etchers such as Ovens, Poorter, Quast—to whom are assigned etchings and drawings that seem to reflect little or no Rembrandt influence. Often the assignments seem arbitrary. Some of the drawings and etchings may be genuine enough, but are representative of a style acquired after the pupils became independent masters.

Renesse belongs in this class. He was with Rembrandt as late as 1649. There is a folio of etchings assigned to him in the British Museum, Sheepshank Collection, but the etchings are hardly Rembrandtesque. They are sketchy and careless, or formal and academic, sometimes free in line like an early Rembrandt or Lievens, and yet never to be confused with either. There are drawings assigned to Renesse in the museums at Amsterdam, Haarlem, Rotterdam, Leipsic, and Vienna, but they furnish no clew to the Rembrandt relation—whatever it was. Doctor Falck (in *Jahrbuch der Preussischen Kunstsammlungen*, Bd. 64, 1925) gives the Annunciation drawing at Berlin (Valentiner, vol. I, 288) to Renesse, with retouchings by Rembrandt, with some probability. He also gives several other drawings to Renesse with perhaps less certainty. There are four drawings in the British Museum which may be considered fairly representative of Renesse just after he left the Rembrandt shop. The Landscape with Archer (Hind, B. M., p. 92) is the best of the four. But none of them is to be mistaken for Rembrandt's work.

ROELAND ROGHMAN
1597–1686

By this landscape-painter and friend of Rembrandt there are many drawings and etchings. There are some twenty-three drawings in the Boymans Museum, Rotterdam, a large number at Haarlem, and two of questionable authenticity in the Louvre, Paris, besides some thirty etchings in the Sheepshank Collection of the British Museum. Both the drawings and etchings show landscapes, townscapes, and seascapes, but few if any of them betray any Rembrandt influence. There is a wash-drawing in the Albertina, Vienna (No. 1381), assigned to Rembrandt that might be given to Roghman. But he is not the man responsible for the so-called Rembrandt landscapes in painting and etching.

PIETER ROTTERMOND
Fl. 1640

There are no paintings extant by Rottermond, who was probably in the Rembrandt shop about 1635 or 1640. A number of signed drawings exist in the museums at Vienna, Amsterdam, and elsewhere. They incline toward the graceful and elegant, but are not without merit. He is best known by his etchings, of which examples may be seen in the Sheepshank Collection of the British Museum, and also in the Ryks Museum, Amsterdam. These etchings are often dotted in the background and faces—the backgrounds a little niggled, and the heads sometimes scratchy or curly in the hair. In the Sheepshank Collection the Jacob and Esau (Rovinski, 77) is signed "Rembrandt f." Some of the drawings which are merely initialled suggest that a confusion of the R's may have led to some of Rottermond's drawings and etchings being mistakenly given to Rembrandt, but it has not been possible for me to identify such work in the Rembrandt *œuvre*. Haden stated that he made etchings with Rembrandt's signature in *facsimile*, but I do not know his authority for that statement.

JAN VICTORS
1620–1676

A number of paintings are rightly given to Victors, but his drawings are scarce. In the British Museum the Old Man Playing (Hind, B. M., p. 94) is possibly by him, and a good drawing. At Amsterdam, in the Ryks Museum, the drawing (given to Rembrandt) Jacob Blessing (Lilienfeld, Amsterdam, 5) is possibly by Victors, though it has features reminiscent of Eeckhout. In the Albertina, Vienna, the drawing of Hagar and Ishmael (H. de G., 1397; Meder, 795) is the study for the picture of the same subject in London trade a few years ago. In my volume on the Rembrandt paintings I gave the picture to Victors. The drawing should likewise be given to Victors, but with the reservation again that both drawing and picture are reminiscent of Eeckhout. Little is known about Victors's life, and what contact, if any, he had with Eeckhout.

JAN GEORG VAN VLIET
1610–?

Van Vliet was probably born at Delft, was a pupil and a shop assistant of Rembrandt at Leyden, and afterward may have followed Rembrandt to Amsterdam. He was an etcher, and, if we are to judge by the etchings now remaining to him, a rather coarse workman. There are about fifty etchings put down to him in the Sheepshank Collection of the British Museum, some of them after supposed designs of Rembrandt (such as the Lot and His Daughters) and others after Lievens and Schooten, with plates of his own design. The plates are small in size, violent in contrasts of black and white, somewhat mannered in the basket-work of the backgrounds, and not subtle or sensitive in the use of line. The conceptions when original are grotesque, especially with such characters as old men and beggars, of which there are a number of plates. These plates of beggars agree with many of the beggar pieces put down among the Rembrandt etchings, and no doubt Van Vliet did many of those sent out from the Rembrandt shop under the Rembrandt name—the better ones as well as the worse ones. Haden thought he reproduced Rembrandt, and was responsible for the "cupboard full of prints by Van Vliet after pictures by Rembrandt" which figured in the Inventory of the Rembrandt bankrupt sale (Haden, p. 23).

In his youth and under Rembrandt, Van Vliet probably worked with greater care than in later years, and there is nothing about the beggar etchings, nothing so good or so bad, that he could not have done. That Rembrandt did them seems almost unthinkable. They reflect neither his mind nor his hand. He was much too serious for the grotesque, and much too sure of hand for the coarse, uncertain cutting which characterizes almost all of the single beggar pieces.

But it is now almost impossible to assign these different etchings to their makers because of the confusion of the record and the misleading signatures and inscriptions. For example, the Old Woman Reading (Sheepshank Collection, 18) is put down to Van Vliet. It is the so-called Rembrandt's Mother, and the painting for it has been recently added to the Ryks Museum, Amsterdam, under the name of Rembrandt. But was the picture done by Rembrandt? A good argument might be made for its Dou origin. Perhaps both picture and etching were of Rembrandt shop origin, and received the Rembrandt name as a trademark, and no more. It is impossible at the present time to be certain about the various shop works of this early seventeenth century. Without wishing to deceive, and following the custom of the time, several hands may have been employed upon a work and thus have bred confusion. Van Vliet's work in etching, as now assigned to him, has a consistency and likeness in method that leaves little doubt of its being by one individual. It is doubtless Van Vliet in his coarser vein. But who shall say that he did not at one time do better work, and that this better work does not now appear under Rembrandt's name in the Rembrandt *œuvre?* It would not be the first time such a substitution has been made.

CHAPTER XII

DRAWINGS AND ETCHINGS BY UNKNOWN PUPILS

I HERE bring together in groups certain drawings and etchings in the Rembrandt *œuvre*, each group, in its conception and workmanship, seeming to indicate an individuality. None of the work in the groups is by Rembrandt, but I am not able to give the name of the pupil or follower that did any one of the groups. There is no lack of names that might be taken from the list of Rembrandt pupils who are to-day without drawings or etchings of any kind, but I prefer to list the groups under letters of the alphabet and allow them to stand separately until perhaps some day the authors may be identified. I followed this course in my volume on the Rembrandt paintings, except that I gave numbers to the groups there where I give letters to the groups here. I hope that eventually I may be able to connect up some of these groups and ascertain their authors. For example, I am now almost persuaded that Unknown Pupil—Group II in my volume on the paintings is none other than Bernaert Fabritius, but I prefer to wait for further evidence before saying so positively.

UNKNOWN PUPIL—GROUP A

The draftsman responsible for this group seems marked by a peculiar dramatic quality in which pathos plays a large part. The half-dozen drawings I am able to assign him are all a bit agonized or tear-stained, or wrung with some mental distress. I cannot find this shown in the same way in any of the other drawings in the Rembrandt *œuvre*. Moreover, the technical workmanship is peculiar and unusual. The drawing is hesitant, weak, rather crude. There is some work with a broad split pen (as in the Hamburg and Paris drawings listed below), some rubbing with the thumb (as in the Berlin drawing given below), some spottiness in the placing of blacks, and some ineffective scratching of foliage. The same workmanship is apparent in all the drawings, also the types and models are the same. The draftsman was probably some weaker brother in the Rembrandt school. The one etching I can assign to him (listed below) indicates he *was* in the school and probably influenced somewhat by Van der Pluym as well as by Rembrandt.

A DRAWINGS GIVEN TO REMBRANDT

BERLIN:
KAISER-
FRIEDRICH
MUSEUM

THE FLIGHT INTO EGYPT
Valentiner, vol. I, 335.

COPENHAGEN
MUSEUM

*JACOB'S DREAM
Valentiner, vol. I, 431.

FRANKFORT:
STAEDEL
INSTITUTE

REUBEN MOURNING FOR JOSEPH
Valentiner, vol. I, 94.

Compare for types and method with the London Morrison drawing (Valentiner, vol. I, 138) and the Berlin drawing (Valentiner, vol. I, 335).

HAMBURG:
KUNSTHALLE

HAGAR AND ISHMAEL
Valentiner, vol. I, 34.

*CHRIST ON THE MOUNT OF OLIVES
Hind, D., XXXI.

A drawing for the etching of the same subject listed hereafter under etchings of the A Group.

LONDON:
MORRISON
COLLECTION

*MANOAH'S SACRIFICE
Valentiner, vol. I, 138.

NEW YORK:
MORGAN
LIBRARY

CHRIST DISPUTING WITH DOCTORS
Valentiner, vol. I, 349.

PARIS:
LOUVRE,
BONNAT
COLLECTION

HAGAR AT THE WELL
Valentiner, vol. I, 16.

DAVID PLAYING BEFORE SAUL
Valentiner, vol. I, 151.

A ETCHINGS GIVEN TO REMBRANDT

AMSTERDAM:
RYKS MUSEUM

*CHRIST ON MOUNT OF OLIVES
Hind, 293.

Excellent in sentiment and effective in its diagonal lines at the back. The background is suggestive of the hand that did the sky in the Three Trees. There is a study for this etching at Hamburg listed above under drawings by Unknown Pupil—Group A (Hind, D., XXXI).

UNKNOWN PUPIL—GROUP B

The draftsman of this group is quite as crude and feeble as the draftsman of Group A. There are a number of these weak pupils or followers that in manner run rather closely together. They are not important and I list only a few of the drawings of each one.

B DRAWINGS GIVEN TO REMBRANDT

DRESDEN
MUSEUM
*SAUL AND DAVID
Lilienfeld, Dresden, 38; Valentiner, vol. I, 152.

PARIS:
LOUVRE,
BONNAT
COLLECTION
*DELILAH AND THE PHILISTINES
Valentiner, vol. I, 143.

PHILADELPHIA:
WIDENER
COLLECTION
*WEDDING OF JOSEPH AND MARY
Valentiner, vol. I, 284.

*HANNAH AND ELI
Valentiner, vol. I, 150.

UNKNOWN PUPIL—GROUP C

Another group of feeble drawings with their grouping not at all certain.
The group is put together tentatively. It is rather closely related to
Group B and to Van der Pluym.

C DRAWINGS GIVEN TO REMBRANDT

BREMEN:
KUNSTHALLE
*THE ANNUNCIATION
Valentiner, vol. I, 287.

THE HAGUE:
H. DE GROOT
COLLECTION
*ANGEL APPEARING TO JOSEPH IN A DREAM
Valentiner, vol. I, 333.

*APPEARANCE TO THE SHEPHERDS
Valentiner, vol. I, 291.

LONDON:
BRITISH
MUSEUM
ISAAC BLESSING JACOB
Valentiner, vol. I, 66.
This drawing may not belong to the group.

PARIS:
LOUVRE,
BONNAT
COLLECTION
*THE UNFAITHFUL SERVANT
Valentiner, vol. I, 364.

UNKNOWN PUPIL—GROUP D

Still another group of weak drawings, recognizable partly by the mannerisms of their background lines.

D DRAWINGS GIVEN TO REMBRANDT

AMSTERDAM:
RYKS MUSEUM
*DEPARTURE OF LOT
Lilienfeld, Amsterdam, 1; Valentiner, vol. I, 36.

MUNICH:
OLD
PINACOTHEK

JOSEPH'S BLOODY COAT
Valentiner, vol. I, 99.

*OLD TOBIT BLINDED
Valentiner, vol. I, 217.*

UNKNOWN PUPIL—GROUP E

This draftsman seems to have an affinity with Flinck rather than Rembrandt. He is perhaps some pupil or follower of Flinck. The drawings are not so uniform in style as in dramatic quality. They are grouped tentatively.

E DRAWINGS GIVEN TO REMBRANDT

BERLIN:
KAISER-
FRIEDRICH
MUSEUM

STANDING ORIENTAL
Lilienfeld, Berlin, 94.

DRESDEN
MUSEUM

*MANOAH'S OFFERING
Valentiner, vol. I, 133.*

ELISHA AND THE SHUNAMITE
Valentiner, vol. I, 189.

FRANKFORT:
STAEDEL
INSTITUTE

SATAN AND CHRIST
Valentiner, vol. I, 351.

THE HAGUE:
H. DE GROOT
COLLECTION

GOD APPEARS TO JOSHUA
Valentiner, vol. I, 128.

*ELISHA AND THE SHUNAMITE
Valentiner, vol. I, 190.*

STOCKHOLM
MUSEUM

A PREACHER
Neumann, 49.

UNKNOWN PUPIL—GROUP F

Bol seems to have had some influence on the draftsman of this group of drawings. The sharp emphasis of the standing figure at the side is a peculiar Bol mannerism, and yet these drawings are hardly by Bol. The mannerism is so marked in the Stockholm drawing as to suggest that the figure of Isaac has been added by a later hand. Even the Lot drawing in the British Museum (Valentiner, vol. I, 40) seems reinforced by a late hand in the woman at the extreme right. The group is problematical, like the ones given above, but its examples indicate a better workmanship.

133. UNKNOWN PUPIL A (GIVEN TO REMBRANDT): DRAWING
OF MANOAH'S SACRIFICE
Morrison Collection, London

134. UNKNOWN PUPIL A (GIVEN TO REMBRANDT): DRAWING
OF JACOB'S DREAM
Copenhagen Museum

135. UNKNOWN PUPIL A (GIVEN TO REMBRANDT): DRAWING
OF CHRIST ON MOUNT OF OLIVES
Hamburg Museum

136. UNKNOWN PUPIL A (GIVEN TO REMBRANDT):
ETCHING OF CHRIST ON MOUNT OF OLIVES
H. 293

PLATE XXXIV

137. UNKNOWN PUPIL B (GIVEN TO REMBRANDT): DRAWING
OF DELILAH AND PHILISTINES
(Bonnat Collection) Louvre, Paris

138. UNKNOWN PUPIL B (GIVEN TO REMBRANDT): DRAWING
OF SAUL AND DAVID
Dresden Museum

139. UNKNOWN PUPIL B (GIVEN TO REMBRANDT): DRAWING
OF JOSEPH AND MARY
Widener Collection, Philadelphia

140. UNKNOWN PUPIL B (GIVEN TO REMBRANDT): DRAWING
OF HANNAH AND ELI
Widener Collection, Philadelphia

PLATE XXXV

141. UNKNOWN PUPIL C (GIVEN TO REMBRANDT): DRAWING
OF ANNUNCIATION
Bremen Kunsthalle

142. UNKNOWN PUPIL C (GIVEN TO REMBRANDT): DRAWING
OF ANGEL APPEARING TO JOSEPH
H. de Groot Collection, The Hague

143. UNKNOWN PUPIL C (GIVEN TO REMBRANDT): DRAWING
OF THE UNFAITHFUL SERVANT
(Bonnat Collection), Louvre, Paris

144. UNKNOWN PUPIL C (GIVEN TO REMBRANDT): DRAWING
OF APPEARANCE TO SHEPHERDS
H. de Groot Collection, The Hague

PLATE XXXVI

145. UNKNOWN PUPIL D (GIVEN TO REMBRANDT): DRAWING
OF DEPARTURE OF LOT
Ryks Museum, Amsterdam

146. UNKNOWN PUPIL D (GIVEN TO REMBRANDT): DRAWING
OF OLD TOBIT BLINDED
Old Pinacothek, Munich

147. UNKNOWN PUPIL E (GIVEN TO REMBRANDT):
DRAWING OF MANOAH'S OFFERING
Dresden Museum

148. UNKNOWN PUPIL E (GIVEN TO REMBRANDT):
DRAWING OF ELISHA AND SHUNAMITE
H. de Groot Collection The Hague

PLATE XXXVII

150. UNKNOWN PUPIL F (GIVEN TO REMBRANDT): DRAWING
OF LOT'S FLIGHT
British Museum, London

149. UNKNOWN PUPIL F (GIVEN TO REMBRANDT): DRAWING
OF HEALING OF TOBIT
Joseph Reinach Collection, Paris

151. UNKNOWN PUPIL G (GIVEN TO REMBRANDT): DRAWING
OF HEALING OF PETER'S MOTHER-IN-LAW
Ryks Museum, Amsterdam

152. UNKNOWN PUPIL G (GIVEN TO REMBRANDT): DRAWING
OF SUPPER AT EMMAUS
Berlin Museum

PLATE XXXVIII

153. UNKNOWN PUPIL H (GIVEN TO REMBRANDT): DRAWING
OF TOBIAS AND FISH
Copenhagen Museum

154. UNKNOWN PUPIL H (GIVEN TO REMBRANDT): DRAWING
OF TOBIAS AND FISH
Königs Collection, Haarlem

155. UNKNOWN PUPIL H (GIVEN TO REMBRANDT): DRAWING
OF TOBIAS AND FISH
Albertina, Vienna

156. UNKNOWN PUPIL H (GIVEN TO REMBRANDT): DRAWING
OF ELIJAH AND RAVENS
H. de Groot Collection, The Hague

PLATE XXXIX

F DRAWINGS GIVEN TO REMBRANDT

HAARLEM:
TEYLER
MUSEUM

CHRIST WITH MARY AND MARTHA
Valentiner, vol. I, 396.
> This drawing is possibly by Bol.

LONDON:
BRITISH
MUSEUM

*LOT'S FLIGHT
Valentiner, vol. I, 40.

PARIS:
J. REINACH
COLLECTION

*HEALING OF TOBIT
Valentiner, vol. I, 252.

STOCKHOLM
MUSEUM

ABRAHAM AND ISAAC
Valentiner, vol. I, 46.

UNKNOWN PUPIL—GROUP G

Here are several drawings by some follower of Bol. The type of Christ with the pale halo back of the head is the first resemblance to be noted. Other analogies can be traced without difficulty.

G DRAWINGS GIVEN TO REMBRANDT

AMSTERDAM:
RYKS MUSEUM

*HEALING OF PETER'S MOTHER-IN-LAW
Lilienfeld, Amsterdam, 13.

AMSTERDAM:
F. MÜLLER
COLLECTION

CHRIST WITH MARY
Valentiner, vol. I, 395.

BERLIN:
KAISER-
FRIEDRICH
MUSEUM

*SUPPER AT EMMAUS
Lilienfeld, Berlin, 66.
> This drawing is not by Rembrandt, and is probably a following after the Louvre picture.

BERLIN:
KAPPEL
COLLECTION

RAISING OF JAIRUS'S DAUGHTER
Valentiner, vol. I, 419.

DRESDEN
MUSEUM

RAISING OF LAZARUS
Lilienfeld, 33; Valentiner, vol. I, 420.

HAARLEM:
KÖNIGS'
COLLECTION

RAISING OF JAIRUS'S DAUGHTER
Valentiner, vol. I, 418.

PARIS:
LOUVRE,
BONNAT
COLLECTION

DAVID ON HIS DEATH-BED
Valentiner, vol. I, 434.

STOCKHOLM
MUSEUM

PILATE AND CHRIST
Michel, vol. II, 95.

UNKNOWN PUPIL—GROUP H

This group of drawings seems related to a group of etchings by a landscapist who appears hereafter under the head of Group I. The work is mannered and feeble. How all these feeble drawings that I am listing under letters of the alphabet could ever have been thought worthy of a great master like Rembrandt seems inexplicable. A Tobias and Fish picture in the Glasgow Corporation Art Gallery seems related to several of the drawings that follow in this H group, in feebleness if not otherwise.

H DRAWINGS GIVEN TO REMBRANDT

COPENHAGEN MUSEUM	*TOBIAS AND THE FISH *Valentiner, vol. I, 236b.*
HAARLEM: KÖNIGS' COLLECTION	*TOBIAS AND THE FISH *Valentiner, vol. I, 237.*
THE HAGUE: H. DE GROOT COLLECTION	*ELIJAH AND THE RAVENS *Valentiner, vol. I, 184.*
PARIS: LOUVRE, BONNAT COLLECTION	TOBIAS AND THE FISH *Valentiner, vol. I, 236a.*
VIENNA: ALBERTINA	*TOBIAS AND THE FISH *Valentiner, vol. I, 238.*

CHAPTER XIII

UNKNOWN LANDSCAPISTS MISTAKEN FOR REMBRANDT

I HAVE here put together in groups certain drawings and etchings of landscape that are not by Rembrandt or any well-known pupils of his school. I cannot identify or name the artists of the different groups. It has been possible only to classify works of a kind and give each group an identifying letter as heretofore. The same method was carried out in my book on the Rembrandt paintings, but the groups there do not correspond to the groups here. To avoid possible confusion, I repeat that the groups here are given a *letter*; in the book on the paintings they were given a *number*. The object of the grouping is, of course, to establish certain artistic personalities, now lost in the Rembrandt *œuvre*, and without a name or place in the history of the school. That there are a number of distinct personalities responsible for the landscapes attributed to Rembrandt has long been vaguely recognized. Fifty years ago Middleton spoke of "the landscapes of a later time so entirely different in their handling." Almost every Rembrandt student has noticed the wide variations in styles.

UNKNOWN LANDSCAPIST—GROUP I

This draftsman used black unmodulated lines, giving an inky appearance to his work. He seems closely related to the draftsman under Group H listed above.

I DRAWINGS GIVEN TO REMBRANDT

AMSTERDAM:
RYKS MUSEUM
*LANDSCAPE WITH HOUSE AND BOAT
Lilienfeld, Amsterdam, 50.

BERLIN:
KAISER-
FRIEDRICH
MUSEUM
*PEASANT COTTAGES
Lilienfeld, Berlin, 166.

TREES AND WATER
Lilienfeld, Berlin, 168.

LANDSCAPE AND PEASANT COTTAGES
Lilienfeld, Berlin, 174.

THE PROPHET ELIJAH
Valentiner, vol. I, 182.
Attribution tentative.

CHATSWORTH: **LANDSCAPE**
DEVONSHIRE *Michel, vol. II, p. 143.*
COLLECTION

LONDON: **LANDSCAPE WITH COTTAGES AND BRIDGE**
BRITISH *Michel, vol. II, p. 58.*
MUSEUM

LANDSCAPE WITH COTTAGE
Hind, B. M., No. 99, p. 39.

LANDSCAPE WITH VILLAGE STREET
Hind, B. M., 102, p. 40.

HOUSE AMID TREES
Hind, B. M., 103, p. 40.
   This corresponds exactly to the etching (given to Rembrandt) reproduced in Hind, 246.

PARIS: **LANDSCAPE WITH TREE AND DYKE**
GAY *Hind, D., VI.*
COLLECTION Corresponding in style to the etching (given to Rembrandt) reproduced in Hind, 246.

I ETCHINGS GIVEN TO REMBRANDT

AMSTERDAM: ***COTTAGE BESIDE CANAL**
RYKS MUSEUM *Hind, 212.*

*LANDSCAPE WITH THREE GABLED COTTAGES
Hind, 246.
   Thought to be by J. Koninck, but the work seems too coarse for him.

UNKNOWN LANDSCAPIST—GROUP J

This group is close to Group I, preceding. A drawing of a Landscape with Canal Bridge in the Albertina (688), given to Rembrandt, seems to belong in this Group J, but I find no other drawings of a similar style in the European print-rooms.

J ETCHINGS GIVEN TO REMBRANDT

AMSTERDAM: **REST IN THE FLIGHT**
RYKS MUSEUM *Hind, 216.*
   This looks like an unfinished etching by Van der Pluym, but tentatively it may be listed here. Note the tree and the two birds—features repeated hereafter in other etchings by this etcher.

158. UNKNOWN PUPIL I (GIVEN TO REMBRANDT): DRAWING
OF LANDSCAPE WITH PEASANT COTTAGES
Berlin Museum

157. UNKNOWN PUPIL I (GIVEN TO REMBRANDT): DRAWING
OF LANDSCAPE WITH HOUSE AND BOAT
Ryks Museum, Amsterdam

159. UNKNOWN PUPIL I (GIVEN TO REMBRANDT): ETCHING
OF COTTAGES BESIDE CANAL
H. 212

160. UNKNOWN PUPIL I (GIVEN TO REMBRANDT): ETCHING
OF LANDSCAPE WITH THREE COTTAGES
H. 246

PLATE XL

161. UNKNOWN LANDSCAPE GROUP J (GIVEN TO REMBRANDT):
ETCHING OF CANAL WITH ANGLER
H. 238

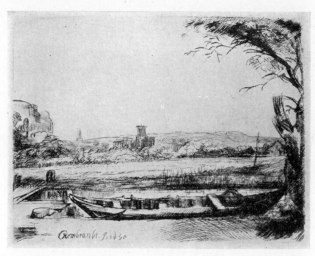

162. UNKNOWN LANDSCAPE GROUP J (GIVEN TO REMBRANDT):
ETCHING OF CANAL WITH BOAT
H. 239

164. UNKNOWN LANDSCAPE GROUP K (GIVEN TO REMBRANDT):
ETCHING OF GOLD–WEIGHERS FIELD
H. 249

163. UNKNOWN LANDSCAPE GROUP K (GIVEN TO REMBRANDT):
ETCHING OF AMSTERDAM
H. 176

PLATE XLI

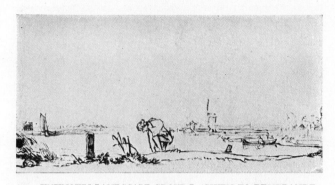

165. UNKNOWN LANDSCAPE GROUP L (GIVEN TO REMBRANDT):
DRAWING OF LANDSCAPE WITH BATHER
Berlin Museum

166. UNKNOWN LANDSCAPE GROUP L (GIVEN TO REMBRANDT):
ETCHING OF SIX BRIDGE
H. 209

167. UNKNOWN LANDSCAPE GROUP M (GIVEN TO REMBRANDT):
ETCHING OF LANDSCAPE WITH COTTAGE
H. 178

168. UNKNOWN LANDSCAPE GROUP M (GIVEN TO REMBRANDT):
ETCHING OF LANDSCAPE WITH COTTAGE
H. 177

PLATE XLII

*Canal with Angler
Hind, 238.

In the style of Hind, 216, above. With two swans.

*Canal with Large Boat
Hind, 239.

It follows the etchings above. Note the tree drawing in Hind, 216, and Hind, 239.

Landscape with Sportsman and Dogs
Hind, 265.

UNKNOWN LANDSCAPIST—GROUP K

This landscapist is one of the best of the numerous etchers that appear in the Rembrandt *œuvre*. There is probably other work by him in the *œuvre*, but I cannot at this time satisfactorily identify more than the two etchings that follow.

K ETCHINGS GIVEN TO REMBRANDT

AMSTERDAM:
RYKS MUSEUM

*View of Amsterdam
Hind, 176.

A little confused in the background and some false values in the foreground, but all told an excellent etching. I am not sure that this and the etching that follows are not by one of the men already listed. But for the present I keep them apart as by an etcher not convincingly identified. There have been copies made of this as of other landscapes attributed to Rembrandt.

*The Gold-Weighers' Field
Hind, 249.

Mr. Pennell insisted that this was the best of the Rembrandt etchings in existence. The statement is strong, but so is the etching. It is not, however, beyond some other etchings listed herein. The light in it is a little glaring and untempered, and it has the defects of the etching above (Hind, 176), but I do not dispute Mr. Pennell's major contention that it is a fine example of the etchings attributed to Rembrandt. Both this and the etching above have a look of Philips de Koninck, especially in their long horizontal lines and repeated planes.

UNKNOWN LANDSCAPIST—GROUP L

Here is a bold and a swift draftsman and a concise etcher. I give to him the celebrated Six Bridge etching (Hind, 209), not because it is not good enough for Rembrandt, and not because I scorn that wonderful story of Rembrandt having done it in a few minutes, but because I find it in agreement with the drawings and etchings put down in this Group L, and not with those of the Rembrandt group.

L DRAWINGS GIVEN TO REMBRANDT

BERLIN:
KAISER-
FRIEDRICH
MUSEUM

*CANAL WITH BATHER
Lilienfeld, Berlin, 167.
> A summary etching, done easily and yet with certainty.

ALLEY OF TREES
Lilienfeld, Berlin, 169.
> Apparently in the manner of Lilienfeld, Berlin, 167, above.

PEASANT HUT WITH ROAD
Lilienfeld, Berlin, 173.

HOUSE AND TREE
Lilienfeld, Berlin, 172.

CHATSWORTH:
DEVONSHIRE
COLLECTION

LANDSCAPE WITH TWO MEN
Lippmann, 53.

ROAD NEAR WATER
Lippmann, 66.

LANDSCAPE, BANKS OF RIVER
Lippmann, 67.

L ETCHINGS GIVEN TO REMBRANDT

AMSTERDAM:
RYKS MUSEUM

*THE SIX BRIDGE
Hind, 209.
> A celebrated etching. The story told by Gersaint is that it was done by Rembrandt, at the house of Jan Six, while a servant went to the village for a pot of mustard that had been forgotten. The etching has more reputation than it deserves. It is good sketch work, freely done, but apparently not done by Rembrandt.

UNKNOWN LANDSCAPIST—GROUP M

The probabilities are that this group landscapist M is identical with one, or perhaps two or more, of the group landscapists given above or hereafter, but I cannot at present find his exact method in any other etching or drawing, so I place these two etchings by themselves.

M ETCHINGS GIVEN TO REMBRANDT

AMSTERDAM:
RYKS MUSEUM

*LANDSCAPE WITH COTTAGE
Hind, 177.

*LANDSCAPE WITH COTTAGE
Hind, 178.
> Excellent etchings, finely done, and with more effect of stippling than of line. They lack somewhat in freedom, but for their kind they are well done.

CHAPTER XIV

OTHER DRAFTSMEN AND ETCHERS MISTAKEN FOR REMBRANDT

HERE follow the names of several painters, draftsmen, and etchers, some of whose works have been arbitrarily assigned to Rembrandt because they happened to be done in a style of the time that later became known as the Rembrandtesque style. The forcing of darks against light, originally derived from the Neapolitan School of Caravaggio, came to Amsterdam before Rembrandt's day. It had been taught by Elsheimer and practised by Bramer, Pynas, and others. It was the common property of the school, and while Rembrandt adopted it and improved upon it, there were others who at different times used it in a way that, to the average person, confused them with Rembrandt. I am now speaking not of Rembrandt's pupils, but of his contemporaries, or those who came just before him. They may have been influenced in their later work by the vogue and method of Rembrandt, but there was abundant opportunity to form themselves in the dark style quite apart from Rembrandt.

I list the names of a few of these men and a few of their works, more to show the possibilities of error in the accepted Rembrandt assignments than to give a complete account of the painters themselves.

JACOB KONINCK OR DE KONINCK
1616?–1708?

Jacob was an older brother and the master of Philips de Koninck, the well-known landscape painter. His dates are uncertain. He seems to have travelled a good deal, was in Norway and Denmark, and in his later life was employed by the royal family at Copenhagen. He was both painter and etcher. Some of his work has come down to us through its being cast out of the Rembrandt *œuvre*. It figures still among the Rejected Rembrandts in the various catalogues. I give a list of his works now recognized, with those taken over from the present Rembrandt *œuvre*, with the understanding that he is still a shadowy character, and his works are subject to revision hereafter.

His method runs close to that of Pieter de With. There were, in fact, half a dozen or more landscapists of the time whose drawings and etchings are much alike. Several of them have been considered already, and several others follow. There is confusion just here, and it is proper to recognize the possibilities of error in attributions. Mr. Turner, in the *Burlington Magazine*, vol. XIV, p. 360, seeks to explain matters as regards Jacob Koninck by saying that he was an eclectic who imitated Van Goyen, Adriaen van de Velde, and others; but that does not seem to clear up the confusion.

DRAWINGS BY JACOB KONINCK

LONDON:
BRITISH
MUSEUM

*VIEW OF RANSDORP
Hind, B. M., 1, p. 80.

This is the original drawing for the etching Hind, 329, among the Rejected Rembrandt etchings. The etching is signed "J. Koninck, 1663," and shows this drawing in reverse. There is no reason to doubt either drawing or etching. They are probably both by Koninck and may be accepted as a criterion of his style.

LANDSCAPE WITH RIVER AND ANGLERS
Hind, B. M., p. 81.

The drawing has on the back the name "J. Cooning," and Mr. Hind accepts the drawing as probably by Koninck. It is somewhat different from the drawing listed above, but may be accepted here tentatively.

ROTTERDAM:
BOYMANS
MUSEUM

TWO LANDSCAPES

These are rather crude drawings and should be accepted only in a very tentative way. They have been assigned to J. Koninck, but the reasons for doing so are not too apparent.

DRAWINGS BY JACOB KONINCK GIVEN TO REMBRANDT

BERLIN:
KAISER-
FRIEDRICH
MUSEUM

*LANDSCAPE
Lilienfeld, Berlin, 175.

It corresponds very closely to the manner of the authenticated drawing by Koninck in the British Museum (Hind, B. M., 1, p. 80) listed above.

*LANDSCAPE
Lilienfeld, Berlin, 170.

CHATSWORTH:
DEVONSHIRE
COLLECTION

LANDSCAPE
Michel, vol. I, p. 241.

LANDSCAPE
Michel, vol. II, p. 166.

169. JACOB KONINCK: DRAWING OF RANSDORP
British Museum, London

170. JACOB KONINCK (GIVEN TO REMBRANDT): DRAWING
OF LANDSCAPE
Berlin Museum

171. JACOB KONINCK (GIVEN TO REMBRANDT): DRAWING
OF LANDSCAPE
Berlin Museum

172. JACOB KONINCK (GIVEN TO REMBRANDT): DRAWING
OF LANDSCAPE
Devonshire Collection, Chatsworth

PLATE XLIII

174. JACOB KONINCK (GIVEN TO REMBRANDT): ETCHING
OF LANDSCAPE WITH TREES
H. 244

173. JACOB KONINCK (GIVEN TO REMBRANDT): ETCHING
OF LANDSCAPE WITH TOWER
H. 245

175. JACOB KONINCK (GIVEN TO REMBRANDT): ETCHING
OF LANDSCAPE WITH ROAD
H. 264

176. JACOB KONINCK (GIVEN TO REMBRANDT): ETCHING
OF CLUMP OF TREES
H. 263

PLATE XLIV

*LANDSCAPE

Michel, vol. II, p. 56.

These three landscape drawings with several others in the Devonshire Collection seem to belong to Jacob Koninck.

DRESDEN
MUSEUM

PEASANT COTTAGE

Lilienfeld, Dresden, 91.

LONDON:
BRITISH
MUSEUM

STUDY OF A CLUMP OF TREES

Hind, B. M., 107, p. 41.

LONDON:
FORMER
HESELTINE
COLLECTION

LANDSCAPE

Michel, vol. I, p. 101.

ETCHINGS BY JACOB KONINCK

LONDON:
BRITISH
MUSEUM

VILLAGE WITH RUINED TOWER

Hind, 329.

This is the etching after the drawing View of Ransdorp listed above. The etching is signed by Koninck and dated 1663. It is no doubt a genuine Koninck, though still listed under Rejected Rembrandts.

ETCHINGS BY JACOB KONINCK GIVEN TO REMBRANDT

LONDON:
BRITISH
MUSEUM

LANDSCAPE WITH OBELISK

Hind, 243.

Note the lines of shading in the foreground and the hatching of the obelisk in connection with the Ransdorp drawing. And yet it has features suggestive of De With.

*LANDSCAPE WITH TREES

Hind, 244.

The trees, thatching, tower, are variations of the Ransdorp drawing.

*LANDSCAPE WITH SQUARE TOWER

Hind, 245.

The plate is much bungled, probably by reworking; but it still has a look common to all the plates here ascribed to Jacob Koninck. Compare with the etching (Hind, 329) listed under Koninck's name above.

*CLUMP OF TREES

Hind, 263.

*LANDSCAPE WITH ROAD

Hind, 264.

VILLAGE WITH TWO GABLED COTTAGES

Hind, 324.

Mr. Hind thinks it perhaps by Koninck and I list it tentatively. It is still among the Rejected Rembrandts.

PIETER DE WITH
Fl. 1659

Pieter de With was a landscape painter and etcher whose work has been given to Rembrandt and others to such an extent that none of his paintings and few of his etchings and drawings now stand under his own name. Almost all of his signed and initialled drawings and etchings are still listed among the Rejected Rembrandts, as though some glint of glory remained to him even in the rejection. I have sorted them out, giving back to him the drawings and etchings apparently by him, and putting down others that may be accepted tentatively. His work is not unlike several landscapists of his time, notably Jacob Koninck.

DRAWINGS BY PIETER DE WITH

LONDON:
BRITISH
MUSEUM

*Landscape with Village and Canal
Hind, B. M., 1, *p. 95.*
 Signed on the back "Pieter de With."

*Landscape with Canal
Hind, B. M., 2, *p. 96.*
 Signed "Rembran" by a late hand. Mr. Hind thinks it by De With, though it has been attributed to Lievens. It is not wholly distinctive and might be by Jacob Koninck. Attribution tentative.

DRAWINGS BY PIETER DE WITH GIVEN TO REMBRANDT

BERLIN:
KAISER-
FRIEDRICH
MUSEUM

*Landscape with Two Men
Lilienfeld, Berlin, 177.
 The drawing of trees, haycocks and the two men, the diagonal road lines, the composition are practically the same as in the De With drawings listed above (Hind, B. M., pp. 95 and 96).

CHATSWORTH:
DEVONSHIRE
COLLECTION

Landscape with Road and Boats
Lippmann, Second Series, 66; *Michel, vol. I, p.* 137.

Sketch of a Landscape
Michel, vol. II, p. 207.
 The drawing, especially in the trunks and foliage of trees, the line of the pen, the compositions seem to relate this drawing with those cited above.

DRESDEN
MUSEUM

*Peasant House
Lilienfeld, Dresden, 130.

Peasant House
Lilienfeld, Dresden, 92.

LONDON:
FORMER
HESELTINE
COLLECTION

View on the Amstel
Heseltine, 25.

177. PIETER DE WITH: DRAWING OF LANDSCAPE WITH
VILLAGE
British Museum, London

178. PIETER DE WITH: DRAWIN
CANAL
British Museum,

179. PIETER DE WITH (GIVEN TO REMBRANDT): DRAWING
OF LANDSCAPE WITH TWO MEN
Berlin Museum

180. PIETER DE WITH (GIVEN TO
OF PEASANT I
Dresden Mus

PLATE XLV

182. PIETER DE WITH (GIVEN TO REMBRANDT): ETCHING OF
LANDSCAPE WITH HAY BARN
H. 241

181. PIETER DE WITH (GIVEN TO REMBRANDT): ETCHING OF
COTTAGE WITH WHITE PALING
H. 203

183. PIETER DE WITH (GIVEN TO REMBRANDT): ETCHING OF
LANDSCAPE WITH MILKMAN
H. 242

184. PIETER DE WITH (GIVEN TO REMBRANDT): ETCHING OF
THREE TREES
H. 205

PLATE XLVI

ETCHINGS BY PIETER DE WITH GIVEN TO REMBRANDT

AMSTERDAM:
RYKS MUSEUM

*LANDSCAPE WITH MILKMAN
Hind, 242.

The pen sketch for this etching—the first idea—is probably the drawing in the British Museum (Hind, B. M., 1, p. 95) by Pieter de With. The etching is also by him, in all probability.

LONDON:
BRITISH
MUSEUM

*COTTAGE WITH WHITE PALING
Hind, 203.

An etching of much excellence—so much that one wonders if De With could reach up to it. And yet it is in his style, his theme, his method of working. It runs close, however, to the manner of Jacob Koninck. There is just now confusion of their styles, and the assignments must be considered as tentative.

*THE THREE TREES
Hind, 205.

To assign the Three Trees to any one other than Rembrandt will, of course, meet with violent dissent. I hasten to add that the assignment is tentative and based almost wholly on the background. No one can base anything on the foreground and sky, because they have been hopelessly muddled by much reworking. The values of almost everything in the composition have been purposely forced and are now confused. The three trees seem to recede, and yet if you put your hand over the trunks you will see that the tops are all of a piece and on the same plane. The sky and rain are purely arbitrary—darkened to force the light in the centre. The distant background is the only good bit left in the plate. This seems in the style of the Cottage with White Paling (Hind, 203) and several other etchings that I shall assign for the moment to De With. Many copies of the Three Trees.

*LANDSCAPE WITH HAY BARN
Hind, 241.

Another excellent etching—there is nothing better of its kind in the Rembrandt *œuvre*. In the style of the Ransdorf drawing by Koninck, and also the Cottage with White Paling listed above. Listed here temporarily because it is too fine to be ignored, and it almost certainly lies between De With and Koninck.

CLUMP OF TREES BESIDE DYKE ROAD
Hind, 327.

Mr. Hind queries if it is not by P. de With. It is among the Rejected Rembrandts.

ORCHARD WITH BARN
Hind, 328.

Initialled "P. D. W." according to Seidlitz. Attributed also to J. Koninck. Among the Rejected Rembrandts.

LOW HOUSE ON CANAL BANK
Hind, 336.

Signed "P. D. W.," but among the Rejected Rembrandts.

LANDSCAPE WITH CANAL
Hind, 338.

Mr. Hind gives it to De With with a query. Wilson thought it by J. Koninck. Apparently in agreement with other plates ascribed to De With.

COTTAGE WITH SQUARE CHIMNEY
Hind, 340.

A little black, but otherwise good work. Probably by P. de With. Among Rejected Rembrandts.

THE VILLAGE STREET
Hind, 344.

Signed "P. D. W." Among Rejected Rembrandts.

UNFINISHED LANDSCAPE
Hind, 345.

Signed "P. D. W." Among Rejected Rembrandts.

LANDSCAPE WITH CANAL
Hind, 346.

Signed "P. D. W." with a query, according to Mr. Hind. Among Rejected Rembrandts.

JAN RUISSCHER
1600?–1650?

The name is sometimes written Ruischer and Rauscher. It is possible that two men are here confused under the one name. The etching bearing the signature J. Ruisscher harks back to the manner of Hercules Seghers, but the drawings are quite different, with certain mannered forms of composition and arching, flowing lines. Houbraken thought him a painter of mountain landscapes, but the drawings are of flat lands, such as Philips de Koninck painted. I list some of the works given to him, with the thought that they may furnish a clew to the identity of the painter.

DRAWINGS BY JAN RUISSCHER

LONDON:
BRITISH
MUSEUM

*VIEW OF OPEN COUNTRY NEAR CLEVES
Hind, B. M., 1, *p.* 93.

*VIEW OF COUNTRY WITH RIVER
Hind, B. M., 2, *p.* 94.

LANDSCAPE WITH TOWN
Hind, B. M., 3, *p.* 94.

I am following Mr. Hind in attributing the three landscapes above listed to Ruisscher.

JAN RUISSCHER DRAWINGS GIVEN TO REMBRANDT
AND OTHERS

AMSTERDAM:
RYKS MUSEUM

*FLAT LANDSCAPE
Lilienfeld, Amsterdam, 53.

Given to Rembrandt. But the drawing and composition are repeated in the British Museum drawing (Hind, B. M., 8, p. 82) given to Philips de Koninck, but more probably by Jan Ruisscher. The British Museum drawing listed below.

ROAD IN THE DUNES
Lilienfeld, Amsterdam, 49.

It is possibly by Ruisscher, but the attribution is tentative.

LONDON:
BRITISH
MUSEUM

*FLAT LANDSCAPE WITH BROAD RIVER
Hind, B. M., 8, p. 82.

The drawing is given to Philips de Koninck. In the style of Jan Ruisscher, whose name has been suggested by Mr. Hind as the possible author. The same kind of drawing as the Amsterdam (Lilienfeld, 53), listed above, and probably a second version by Ruisscher.

ETCHINGS BY JAN RUISSCHER

LONDON:
BRITISH
MUSEUM,
SHEEPSHANK
COLLECTION

FLAT LANDSCAPE

This is signed J. Ruisscher 1649. Another etching in the same collection is signed Johannes Ranscher F. E. I., and Mr. Hind thinks this and a third etching, signed Ioannes Ruischer Fecit 1649 (Brunswick), are by the same hand as the first one listed. The work of Ruisscher needs further illustration before any conclusion is reached.

HERCULES SEGHERS, OR SEGERS
1589–1645

To Seghers, perhaps, more than to any other Dutch landscapist, has been assigned disputed Rembrandt landscapes. The famous Mill has been declared of Seghers origin, but the reasons for the declaration are not given. The more Seghers is studied the less like Rembrandt he appears. He was an older painter much admired by Rembrandt, and doubtless had some influence upon Rembrandt, but, if we are to believe the drawings and etchings assigned to each of them, they went their separate ways. The drawings given to Seghers in the Louvre Collection are finely finished, exactly drawn, and of much excellence. The many etchings given to him in the Ryks Museum and in the British Museum are minutely drawn, with dots and spots, in a manner wholly singular in the school, and not to be confused with Rembrandt's manner. They are printed on drab-colored papers, and in this respect are again distinctive. Moreover, I do not find any close agreement between his etchings and drawings and paintings and the paintings of landscapes which Doctor Bode has attributed to him. Seghers is to me a man who is not so much confused with Rembrandt as with Koninck and other contemporary artists. Still some of his work may have gotten into the Rembrandt *œuvre*, and I list his name here merely as one of the possibilities to be reckoned with hereafter when definitive history is written. The etching the Flight Into Egypt, attributed to Seghers, originally a Tobias and Angel, and said to have been changed into a Holy Family by Rembrandt, is well known, and has been much discussed. The change was probably made by some shop worker. It is hardly believable that Rembrandt would spend much time and labor altering some other etcher's plate. The liberty taken with the plate—the change itself—indicates merely a shop trick with a possible sale of the prints as a motive. If one should hazard a guess, it would be to the effect that the original Tobias and Angel plate, as regards the figures, lies nearer to Lastman than Seghers, or at the least some one following perhaps Lastman's Tobias and Angel in the Lippmann Collection, Berlin (reproduced in Freise, *Pieter Lastman*, Plate 10).

PIETER LASTMAN
1583–1633

Lastman was Rembrandt's master, and it would be quite natural for Rembrandt in his early days to reflect the teaching and manner of his master, but the influence, such as it was, is not very apparent in the pupil's work. It would seem almost impossible for the works of the two men to be confused, and yet there are Lastman drawings doing service as Rembrandts. They are not numerous and are so obviously not of Rembrandt origin that one wonders how they ever got into such a false position. Under Lastman's name I can find few drawings in the European museums that are at all convincing. In the Louvre are two landscapes with Lastman written at the top, but the name was probably put in by some collector as an aid to memory. Nothing in the drawings suggests Lastman to me. But there are several very obvious drawings by Lastman in the Rembrandt *œuvre*. I take them out and list them.

As for Lastman's etchings, there are a few in existence, such as the Judah and Tamar, etched after Lastman by Pieter Nolpe (Rovinski, 432), an example of which is in the Sheepshank Collection, British Museum, but they are in no way like the Rembrandt etchings, and need not be considered here. For those who would delve into Lastman, there is a volume by

186. JAN RUISSCHER: DRAWING OF COUNTRY WITH RIVER
British Museum, London

185. JAN RUISSCHER: DRAWING OF OPEN COUNTRY NEAR
CLEVES
British Museum, London

187. JAN RUISSCHER (GIVEN TO PHILIPS DE KONINCK):
DRAWING OF FLAT LANDSCAPE
British Museum, London

188. JAN RUISSCHER (GIVEN TO REMBRANDT): DRAWING OF
FLAT LANDSCAPE
Ryks Museum Amsterdam

PLATE XLVII

189. PIETER LASTMAN: PAINTING OF SUSANNA AND ELDERS
Berlin Museum

190. PIETER LASTMAN (GIVEN TO REMBRANDT): DRAWING
OF SUSANNA AND ELDERS
Berlin Museum

191. PIETER LASTMAN (GIVEN TO REMBRANDT): DRAWING
OF MERCURY AND ARGUS
Dresden Museum

192. PIETER LASTMAN (GIVEN TO REMBRANDT): DRAWING
OF JUNO, ARGUS, AND IO
Berlin Museum

PLATE XLVIII

Kurt Freise (*Pieter Lastman, sein Leben und seine Kunst*, Leipzig, 1911) that will prove interesting. He gives to Lastman many pen drawings with probability, but denies to him two drawings in red chalk, listed hereafter, and describes them as copies by Rembrandt after Lastman. I cannot follow him here. The red-chalk drawings are apparently by Lastman— the first sketches for pictures that followed in course.

DRAWINGS BY PIETER LASTMAN GIVEN TO REMBRANDT

AMSTERDAM:
FODOR
MUSEUM

MARS AND VENUS
Weisbach, Pl. 58.

A diagonal composition peculiar to Lastman, with several groups of figures. Attribution tentative.

BERLIN:
KAISER-
FRIEDRICH
MUSEUM

*SUSANNA AND ELDERS
Lilienfeld, Berlin, 31; Weisbach, Pl. 67.

This drawing has been spoken of herein (p. 5). Obviously it is a drawing for Lastman's picture in the Kaiser-Friedrich Museum of the same name. Given to Rembrandt because of some memoranda on the back of it supposed to be in Rembrandt's handwriting. He (Rembrandt) is thought to have made this drawing after the picture, but it is not an accurate copy. Nor is it a copy of any kind. It has the appearance of a free, sketchy memorandum. The composition is slightly varied, something that a copyist very seldom attempts, but a thing a master almost always does, making an improvement in the painting upon his first thought in the drawing. The drawing is not at all in Rembrandt's manner. There is no likeness to it anywhere in the *œuvre*, except in the drawings that follow here.

*JUNO, ARGUS, AND IO
Lilienfeld, Berlin, 77.

Here is Lastman again with his diagonal composition, his classical subject, his types, and his handling of line. It is a pen drawing, but may be compared with the Susanna (listed above), which is in red chalk. Note the heads and profiles of the Argus and the Elder at right; also the legs of Argus and the legs of Susanna should be compared.

SCIPIO AND AFRICAN BRIDE
Lilienfeld, Berlin, 83.

Somewhat in the style of Eeckhout. The subject is also his, as indicated by two pictures, one at the Old Pinacothek, Munich, and the second in the New York Historical Society Collection. But the probabilities favor this drawing being by Lastman.

DRESDEN
MUSEUM

*MERCURY AND ARGUS
Lilienfeld, Dresden, 109a.

In the style of the Berlin drawing (Lilienfeld, 77) and corresponding to Lastman's other drawings here listed.

LONDON:
SOUTH
KENSINGTON
MUSEUM

METAMORPHOSIS OF IO
Dyce, 430.

 With two peacocks and a cow, as in Lilienfeld, Berlin, 31 and 77, given above. Io under a canopy. In ink and wash.

PARIS:
LOUVRE,
BONNAT
COLLECTION

PAUL AND BARNABAS
Reproduced in Freise, "Pieter Lastman," Pl. 12.

 The drawing by Lastman for the picture of the same subject in Count Stetski's Collection, but the drawing is given to Rembrandt as a copy by him after the Lastman picture. It is of the same quality and technique as the Berlin Susanna drawing (Lilienfeld, Berlin, 31), and is not like a copy but a free sketch. Again the sketch varies in detail from the picture, which would hardly be the case were it a copy, but *would* be the case were it an original sketch.

SALOMON SAVRY, OR SAVERY
1594–1664

 An Amsterdam engraver and etcher who did a number of etchings after Rembrandt's pictures, and also made copies of a number of so-called Rembrandt etchings. Haden said that he etched beggars "which are freely signed with Rembrandt's name, with the one exception of the Rat Catcher, the copy of which he avows" (Haden, p. 26). He is also supposed to have etched the "t'is Vinnich Kout" (Hind, 114) and "Das Niet" (Hind, 115), which are certainly not by Rembrandt. Even the designs for these are supposed to be not Rembrandt's but Beham's. Wurzbach (vol. 2, p. 448) gives a list of Savery's etchings after Rembrandt. He was probably responsible for some of the crude beggar etchings put down to Rembrandt, and with his copies no doubt helped to confuse the Rembrandt record.

SIMON DE VLIEGER
1601–1653

 Simon de Vlieger is generally known as a sea painter, but he did portraits, landscape, and *genre*, and etched many plates, some of them still under his name. Rembrandt perhaps admired his work, for in the Rembrandt Inventory made for the bankrupt sale appears the entry "64 Een graeuwtie van Sÿmon de Vlieger." In my volume on the Rembrandt paintings I endeavored to show that the Good Samaritan picture in the Wallace Museum, London, attributed to Rembrandt, was really done by Simon de Vlieger. The etching of this picture follows the picture, and was evidently done from it by some shop etcher, perhaps in Rembrandt's shop. I list the etching under Vlieger's name merely to indicate that he was the inventor, not the etcher.

LONDON:
BRITISH
MUSEUM

THE GOOD SAMARITAN
Hind, 101.

A much overworked etching, certainly not by Rembrandt, and almost as certainly not by Simon de Vlieger, though done after his picture. Everybody doubts this work as a Rembrandt, notwithstanding the voluminous signature, "Rembrandt inventor et fecit, 1633." Haden thought it by Bol. Middleton said it was by the etcher of the Flight into Egypt (Hind, 105), which is quite possible. "The barrel in the corner without substance, rotundity, or containing power, the straw above it like hair; the landscape, buildings, and foliage in the middle distance Rembrandtesque but not Rembrandt" (Haden, p. 36). There are drawings related to this etching in the Louvre, the British Museum, Boymans Museum, Rotterdam (Valentiner, vol. I, 378–380), but I cannot assign them to De Vlieger, or to any other draftsman with certainty.